Vicksburg and the War

Vicksburg and the War

By Gordon A. Cotton
and Jeff T. Giambrone

PELICAN PUBLISHING COMPANY
Gretna 2004

The word "Pelican" and the depiction of a pelican are trademarks
of Pelican Publishing Company, Inc., and are registered
in the U.S. Patent and Trademark Office.

Library of Congress Cataloging-in-Publication Data

Cotton, Gordon A., 1936-
 Vicksburg and the war / by Gordon A. Cotton and Jeff T. Giambrone.
      p. cm.
Includes bibliographical references.
 ISBN 1-58980-171-7 (alk. paper)
 1. Vicksburg (Miss.)—History—Civil War, 1861-1865. 2. Vicksburg (Miss.)—
History—Siege, 1863. 3. Vicksburg (Miss.)—History—Civil War, 1861-1865—
Sources. 4. United States—History—Civil War, 1861-1865—Sources. I.
Giambrone, Jeff T. II. Title.
 F349.V6 C68 2003
 973.7'344—dc22

                                                    2003019500

Printed in Korea

Published by Pelican Publishing Company, Inc.
1000 Burmaster Street, Gretna, Louisiana 70053

CONTENTS

But after all histories are written and the tongue of the last survivor is stilled in death, the Recording Angel will have sealed a heavy volume and labeled it The Untold Sufferings of Vicksburg's Siege.

—William Pitt Chambers
Company B, 46th Mississippi Infantry

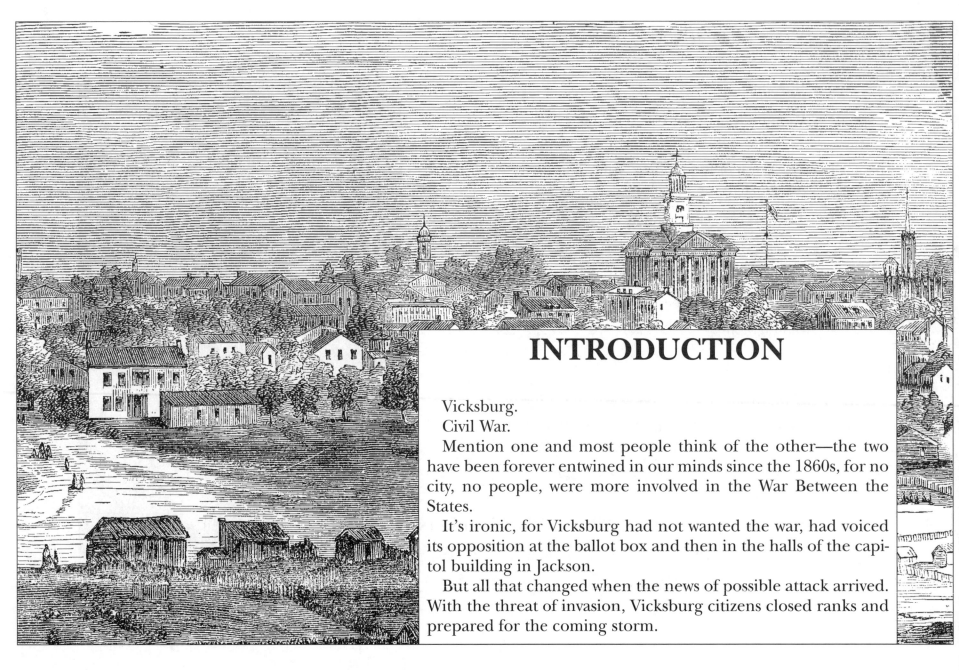

INTRODUCTION

Vicksburg.

Civil War.

Mention one and most people think of the other—the two have been forever entwined in our minds since the 1860s, for no city, no people, were more involved in the War Between the States.

It's ironic, for Vicksburg had not wanted the war, had voiced its opposition at the ballot box and then in the halls of the capitol building in Jackson.

But all that changed when the news of possible attack arrived. With the threat of invasion, Vicksburg citizens closed ranks and prepared for the coming storm.

Vicksburg ungrudgingly gave her support to the war effort not only in materials but also in manpower, filling positions all the way from the presidency of a new nation to over 2,500 soldiers in the ranks—men who marched away to fight for the Confederacy, hundreds of whom never came back.

Many thought the war would last only a few weeks and that the fighting would never reach Vicksburg—but when the roar of cannons echoed across the hills of home, it wasn't a battle that lasted a few hours or, perhaps, a day or more, as in most places. It was a campaign that included numerous engagements that lasted for months and months then culminated in forty-seven days of siege, followed by years of enemy occupation often more odious than the carnage of the battlefield.

It was not just the army and navy and the officials of the Confederacy that we had in mind in compiling this volume of pictures, drawings, and stories—it is the role of the people who kept the Southern flag aloft in their hearts long after the hope of victory was gone. They may have been beaten on the battlefield, but they were never defeated in spirit.

When Gen. John C. Pemberton surrendered, he was speaking for the army, not for the civilians. They might have been forced into their roles, but once they had taken their stand, they were never found wanting in support of the Cause.

Today Vicksburg is the most Southern of cities where a heroic heritage has not been forgotten.

The Evening Citizen.

J. M. SWORDS, Publisher and Proprietor

TERMS PER ANNUM—Daily Paper, $10.00
Weekly Paper, $3.00

Tuesday Evening Feb. 12, 1861.

The Daily Evening Citizen is the only paper in the city that is published every day in the week, by which superior advantages are offered to the advertising public.

JEFFERSON DAVIS,

Of Mississippi,

PRESIDENT

OF THE

SOUTHERN CONFEDERACY.

A. H. STEPHENS,

Vice President.

GEN. JEFFERSON DAVIS,

President of the Southern Republic.

On his way to Montgomery.

FIRST GRAND RECEPTION
AT VICKSBURG.

Mr. Davis having been notified by a telegraphic dispatch on Saturday last of his election as President of the Southern Confederacy, prepared at once to start en route for Montgomery, and taking passage on the magnificent steamer Natchez, he arrived at Vicksburg about half past 2 o'clock yesterday. An immense concourse of people had gathered on the levee to give him a hearty welcome. The booming of cannon, the rattle of musketry, and the shouts of the multitude announced the approach of the steamer, and cheer upon cheer resounded over the hills and over the bosom of the father of waters as the venerable statesman made his appearance before the hosts of

President of the Southern Republic.

In the selection of a person for President of the Southern Republic the Congress at Montgomery acted with great wisdom in its choice of the man for this position. Jeff __ is a statesman, a scholar and a sol__ __ __ directed for military life. served __ __ regular army of the United Stat__ __ first of the 1st infantry and th__ __ Dragoons, and as adjutant in the __ __ Twenty-five years ago he resig__ __ army, and devoted himself to civil occupations and studies. He was elected to Congress in 1845, and resigned to become colonel of the first volunteer regiment of Mississippi Ri__ the Mexican war, and __ __ greatly in his services t__ __ bravery. He led his reg__ __ of Monterey, and was se__ __ battle of Buena Vista.

Declining the appoi__ __ General, he returned to C__ __ from the State of Mississip__ __ until appointed by Mr. I__ __ War. In that office he mai__ __ tion he had previously acqu__ __ extraordinary administrativ__ __ firmness in what he believed __ __ unquestionable, and his integ__ __ taint of suspicion. When Mr. __ __ ceeded Mr. Pierce, Mr. Davis r__ __ Senate, and held his place ther__ __ tenure of the unlimited confiden__ ple of his State. He is eminentl__ __ grasp and character of his mind __ his temperament and his unsullied __ be the organizer of a new admini__ __

In the politics of past times, Mr__ __ belonged, for a long time, to the St__ wing of the Democratic party. In __ phrase of the day, he has been __ classed as a fire-eater. But it is a gr__ of language to apply such an epith__ Davis. A zealous and, if you please,__ supporter of the constitutional rights of the South, his course has been calm, reasoning and dignified, and up to the moment when secession came, in his judgment, to be the last and necessary resource for self protection, he was for fighting the battles of the constitution under the constitution, and in the Union. He clung to the Union hopefully when many others, not more firm in their devotion to Southern rights,

Burning of the Vicksburg Packet
STEAMER CHARMER!

So far as is known five lives were lost, viz: Mr. Ambrose Davis, of Tennessee, and his lovely young __ __ __ __ __ __ __ __ __ __ been thought to have __ __ __ __ __ Orleans; and one of __ __ __ by. One female is __ __ of Mr. Green was __ __ me mile and a half __ __ __ ives the following __ __ __ ree or four of us __ __ he clerk's office, __ __ On looking round __ __ n the ladies' cab__ __ se the sleepers; __ __ roused. But it __ __ ut two weeks __ __ of age, must __ __ r the alarm __ __ not be found, __ __ learn where __ __ though sup__ __ house. The __ __ y, rounding __ __ e point, __ __ t to shatter __ __ ving a gap __ __ __ od many __ __ sly hurt. __ __ contents __ __ __ ylvania, __ __ feared __ __ man of __ __ __ delicate __ __ look__ __ __ an, he __ __ __, but on finding the __ __, turned, poor lady, to arouse __ __ husband, and clung to him with such force that, the watchman says, he could not save her. The smoke became so dense that he had to leave her to save himself. Still, they may pos__ __ __ __ __ __

A Card from Gen

The following card from__ dent of the famous K. __ who is at present sojourn __

K. G.

__ville Courier
Jan. 20th
__shed in the
__ands an ans-
__exan" has __
__C. was intro__
__ization of M
__d States Gov.
therefore, he has concluded __
by misrepresenting the order with what I wish to say to thi__ I beg also to reply to the L__ which published an incend__ weeks ago, in which the K. was greatly misrepresent__

I deny, and will un__ exposition of our doc__ has any affiliation wit__ deny that I ever made __ my life, (but do not pr__ did canvass Texas in the __ ical grounds. I refer him __ the following named gentl__ declaration: Gov. Sam H__ Clarke, Thos. Lubbock, Jol__ Gov. E. S. Lubbock, Col. B__ W. Edwards, Gen. Chappell __ Esq., Judge Ochiltree, and __ nent citizens of Texas, wel__ public.

If to stand up and plea__ al rights of the South; __ white man is better than __ this continent belongs to __ and to open up new ave__ sober working man, is __ the United States Gov__ guilty.

The K. G. C. sprang __ 1854—It has adhered __ succeed, in defiance __ tion that may be heap__ tution, even in Louisvi__ first to respond when a __ ers of the State. It h__ to South Carolina, __ she needs them : __ Government 135,__ not one to fight

Now, sirs, I h__ stood. We look __ of Mexico; yet the __ a paramount duty. __ movement get on __

The arrival of Jefferson Davis in Vicksburg on his way to the presidential inauguration in Montgomery was announced by the *Evening Citizen* on February 12, 1861. Imposed over a copy of the paper is a photograph of Davis taken in 1860.

Preceding pages: Vicksburg as it appeared in an 1863 sketch. The view is looking south, possibly from Fort Hill. (Courtesy Old Court House Museum Collection, hereafter noted as OCHM)

VICKSBURG RAISES THE STARS AND BARS

I hope that our separation may be peaceful. But whether it be so or not, I am ready, as I have always been, to redeem my pledge to you and the South by shedding every drop of my blood in your cause.

—Jefferson Davis
at Vicksburg
February 11, 1861

Smartly dressed soldiers escorted the tall, handsome man from the steamboat as an immense concourse of people crowded the landing, and all local militia units stood at attention as the honored guest was officially welcomed by Robert Crump, mayor of the city of Vicksburg.

The date was Monday, February 11, 1861, and the occasion was the first public appearance of Jefferson Davis as president-elect of the Confederate States of America. In a brief, impromptu address, Davis recounted his attachment to the Old Union, noting that he had worked to maintain "the constitutional equality of all States. . . . We have failed. You and I have resolved that our safety and honor required us to dissolve our connection with the United States."

Only two days earlier, on February 9, Davis had been pruning roses in the tranquility of his garden at Brierfield, his plantation home several miles south of Vicksburg, when he received word of his selection as provisional president of the new republic formed

I.

There Shall Be

War and Rumors of War

—Matthew 24:6

[See page 11.]

The messenger with the notification that Mr. Davis had been elected President. . . . found him in our garden assisting to making rose-cuttings; when reading the telegram he looked so grieved that I feared some evil had befallen our family. After a few minutes' painful silence he told me, as a man might speak of a sentence of death. . . . He assembled his negroes and made them an affectionate farewell speech, to which they responded with expressions of devotion, and he left home next day for Montgomery.

—Varina Davis
Jefferson Davis, A Memoir

Brierfield, the Warren County home of Jefferson and Varina Davis
(Jones, *Davis Memorial Volume*)

by delegates from the seceding states at Montgomery, Alabama. He had not wanted the presidency, but with an admirable military background and a distinguished political career, he was the natural and unanimous choice.

Never one to shirk duty, Davis accepted the task and made immediate preparations to go to Montgomery. Celebrating had already begun in Vicksburg, for as soon as the news reached the city, cannons at the Jackson Street landing boomed, announcing "a new era in the history of nations," James M. Swords, editor of the *Vicksburg Evening Citizen,* wrote. Though there were less than two days to plan a proper ceremony, when Davis arrived to the salute of cannon fire, the rattle of musketry, a military escort, music, and an official welcome, Swords felt the festivities "commensurate with the occasion" for "the greatest and noblest man of the age."

To Davis, the greatest honor was the spontaneous gathering of the enthusiastic throng by "those who have known me best and longest—my old friends and neighbors." As he made his way to the carriage that would take him to the railroad station, bells rang and the crowd cheered their local son who would steer the course of the new nation.

Vicksburg residents had made a sharp turn in political sentiments in only a few months. Usually Whig in sentiment, local voters had chosen Constitutional Union Party candidate John Bell of Tennessee over Southern Democrat John C. Breckinridge 816 to 580 in the presidential election in November 1860. Northern Democrat Stephen A. Douglas had received only 83 votes, which was 83 more than were won by Abraham Lincoln, who failed to score a single endorsement. On the eve of the election, Davis led a torchlight rally for the Breckinridge ticket, but Vicksburg held firm for the Union. When the national results were known,

Vicksburg, April 20th. 1861.

100,000 REWARD!

I WILL give the above reward for the head of ABRAHAM LINCOLN, if taken alive, or 50,000 if taken dead and delivered to me, at Vicksburg, in time for me to hand it over to President Davis, by the 4th of July, next. All the papers please copy.

april 20. d.&w 1t.   RICHARD PRYOR.

An ad in the *Evening Citizen* left no doubt of the attitude of one local resident, Dr. Richard Pryor, about Abraham Lincoln. Lincoln was so disliked that his name was not even put on the ballot in Mississippi. (OCHM)

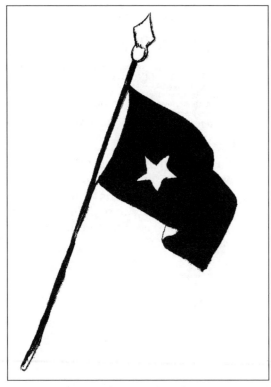

Miss Florence Lightcap of Vicksburg illustrated her autograph book with patriotic drawings, including *The Bonnie Blue Flag*. The book is from the Old Court House Museum Collection in Vicksburg.

Southern Unionists pondered the future, their loyalties torn. Marmaduke Shannon, longtime editor of the *Vicksburg Weekly Whig*, wrote that he would stand by the Union, the Constitution, and its laws, that he would not rebel against the government simply "because an obnoxious man has been made President."

Vicksburg was one of only a few pockets of Union sentiment in Mississippi, and though Bell had made an impressive showing, Breckinridge had carried the state, and clamors for secession were growing. To offset the advocates of disunion, a statewide rally was held in Vicksburg in late November, where speakers counseled patience, advising that problems be solved within the bounds of the Union. The legislature, however, called for an election of delegates to decide Mississippi's ties to the United States, and Vicksburg, remaining true and steadfast, sent Unionist candidates Thomas A. Marshall and Walker Brooke to Jackson; they garnered 561 votes to only 173 for the advocates of secession.

At the convention, Brooke introduced several measures to stall what was, perhaps, inevitable, but when his suggestions were defeated, he told the other delegates that he had "endeavored to carry out the view of my constituents" but had failed and felt it was his painful duty to cast his vote for secession. Marshall did not waver in his refusal to sanction the move but joined with Brooke in reluctantly signing his name to the document as a delegate.

Even the editor of the *Whig* changed his stance. Shannon wrote that Mississippi had spoken, had declared its independence, and though he did not approve it, secession was an accomplished fact. "We, too, take our position by its side," he editorialized. "We stand ready to defend her rights and to share her fate."

Newspapers were full of stories, some factual, many conjecture, which helped to create an atmosphere of alarm. One such story was that Northern abolitionists planned to send steamboats loaded with volunteers to attack Southern ports along the Mississippi River. One such vessel, a boat familiar to the people of Vicksburg, was the *Silver Wave,* said to be on her way.

If there were any misgivings or second thoughts about the state's course of action, such rumors helped to solidify the people, and the mood changed from one of stoicism to martial fervor in a matter of hours on January 11, 1861, the day the *Silver Wave* was expected. Bells rang in alarm, and a militia unit was rushed to Fort Hill, where there was a commanding view of a sweeping curve in the river just north of the city. By the time the men had four cannons in place, troops from nearby Bovina and Edwards Station joined them.

The next evening, a steamboat rounded the bend at DeSoto Point, opposite Vicksburg, and the sound of shots broke the silence on the cold winter night as shells passed across the bow, splashing into the muddy waters of the Mississippi. The vessel wasn't the *Silver Wave* but was the *A. O. Tyler,* whose captain, John Collier, well known in the city, wondered what the fuss was all about and was probably in disbelief when armed troops boarded his boat to search for weapons.

The tiny Republic of Mississippi was only four days old, but it had already flexed its military muscle, three0 months before action in Charleston Harbor would officially start the war.

Despite the scare, the idea of a war was an exaggeration in the minds of many, and even if one did occur, it would surely be over in a matter of weeks. Nevertheless, calls were made for volunteers, and on March 12, the Vicksburg Sharpshooters became the first to reach their quota. A few days later, along with the Vicksburg Artillery, they were mustered into service. They remained for a time in Vicksburg, and another company, the Hill City Cadets, was the first to leave for possible military action. Early on the morning

When soldiers at Vicksburg fired on a steamboat January 12, 1861, it was possibly the first shot of the war in the western part of what became the Confederate States. *(Official and Illustrated War Record)*

of March 27, just as day was breaking, they marched to the railroad depot, escorted by other troops and cheered by a crowd of civilians as they were deployed to protect Confederate interests at Pensacola, Florida. The men broke ranks, took on board extra clothing and food, and bade goodbye to their loved ones before the train pulled out of the station at six o'clock. Such departures in the early months of the war were always festive occasions. The Volunteer Southrons were feted with a dinner and dance the night before they left, and the Jefferson Davis Guards marched off to war with bouquets decorating their bayonets. Often there was the formal and emotional presentation of a company flag, hand-sewn by some of the wives, mothers, and sweethearts, on Court Square.

Proud fathers, tearful wives and mothers, along with envious young boys turned out as each unit left the city. Still, few expected armed conflict. Vicksburg's mayor, only a week before war began in earnest at Fort Sumter, expected the Confederacy to take its place "among the Independent nations of the earth with every prestige of peace, prosperity and happiness." His view was shared by many, while others clamored for a fight. Patriotism was at a fever pitch, with shops stocking Confederate letter paper, envelopes, cards, photographs, badges, and rosettes bearing like-nesses of "Our First President." Only when firing began in South Carolina on April 12, 1861, did citizens acknowledge the probability of all-out war, and even then, it seemed far away. Vicksburg resident Anne Harris wrote in later years, "The first mutterings of war were like a low, rumbling thunder that one hears on a quiet summer day, when there is hardly a cloud to be seen in the sky."

While the firing on Fort Sumter helped unify the North, the calls for men by both governments dashed any hopes for peace or reconciliation. Southerners knew that the peaceful separation

Stand firmly by your cannon,
Let your ball and grapeshot fly;
Trust in GOD and DAVIS,
But "keep your powder dry."

Patriotic stationary, such as the letter-head shown here from the Old Court House Collection, was very popular in the South.

[See page 17.]

I never saw anything like the reception we met with all along the route, particularly in Alabama in this state, and our own, some parts of Tennessee let us pass by very coolly. The ladies all along the route met us by hundreds showering flowers on us at every station, cheering and waving their handkerchiefs. At many places they gave us Strawberries. . . . little notes, verses, etc., one of which I send you in this, also a little flag presented me with a very fine Boquet by Miss Hebron. . . . After we got here, we marched up to President Davis' Hotel and he came out and Reviewed us, and made a short speech. we then marched to Capitol Square, and marched around the statue of Washington, with uncovered heads, from there we went to the Governors Mansion and were invited in had a fine time there, every body says we are the finest company that has come here yet. the city papers are complimenting us all the time.

—Lt. Thomas Jefferson Hanes
Company A, 21st Mississippi Infantry
Richmond, Virginia
June 6, 1861

This little flag, shown only a fraction smaller than the original, was presented to Lt. Thomas Jefferson Hanes by a Miss Hebron. (OCHM)

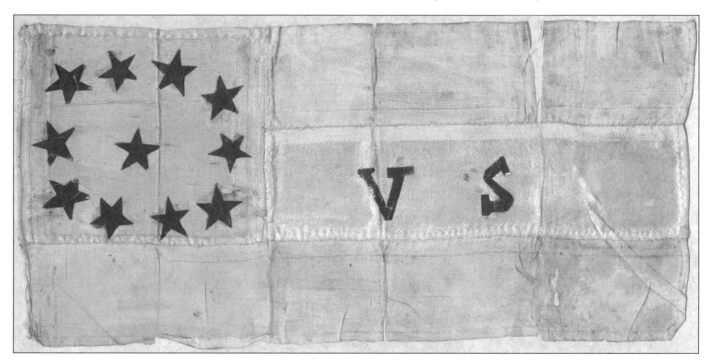

Mississippi troops, pictured in the *London Illustrated News,* wore badges that read "Victory or Death," the same motto on the flag of the Vicksburg Artillery (upper right), which is displayed in the Old Court House Museum. (Cotton Collection)

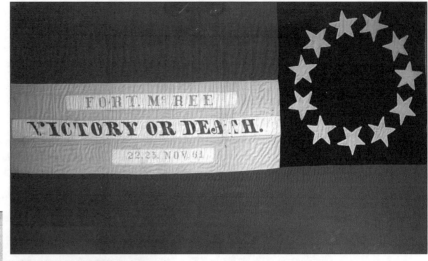

that had been hoped for was a pipe dream, for Lincoln termed their desire for independence a rebellion and determined to crush it.

Everywhere throughout the Confederate States people prepared for war. In Vicksburg the city council appropriated $5,000 for local defense. Six volunteer companies were soon organized (eventually Vicksburg would furnish a dozen), many of those enlisting being men of Northern or foreign birth. There was a brisk sale of bonds to help finance the war, the first ones being bought by Henry Lee and William Newman; both were free men of color. Women organized sewing societies to make uniforms and other items for the soldiers, and classes were offered to teach ladies how to handle a gun.

If anyone had doubts that the Confederacy was a functioning nation, they were reminded by a notice in the *Evening Citizen* that United States postage stamps would no longer be honored when mailing a letter.

War had begun, and yet it seemed to be at a stalemate as spring turned to summer. When the two sides finally met in a pitched battle in Virginia, which Southerners called Manassas and the Yankees named Bull Run, the fact that it was a Confederate victory was no surprise to many; it underscored the belief that the war would soon be over, that the Yankees either couldn't or wouldn't fight.

The newspapers printed dispatches from the front, along with letters from local boys, but about the only war effort in Vicksburg, it seemed, was Reading's and Paxton's foundries, casting cannons to be used far away, and trains rumbling through town crowded with troops headed to the scenes of action.

There may have been no sounds of war in Vicksburg, but there were some reminders other than casualty lists printed in the local

Capt. Felix Hughes organized the Sarsfield Southrons, Company C, 22nd Mississippi Infantry, in 1861. He was killed while leading the regiment in the Battle of Baton Rouge, August 5, 1862. His portrait was painted posthumously by J. Travis Smith from a small photograph in 1887. It is in the collections of the Old Court House Museum in Vicksburg.

papers. Some families, whose main providers had answered the call to arms, were in need. The city council appropriated funds for fuel and food, and the Confederate government supplied Military Relief Warrants, which were vouchers for fuel, food, and rent, usually for needy widows or families of men in service. Citizens also organized a Free Market, where food was provided for about a hundred families.

The first Confederate Christmas was like springtime, with flowers blooming on the warm, sunny days. The Hill City Cadets were home on furlough, and the war moved at a snail's pace on the eastern seaboard.

As the conflict went on, scarcity became more evident on the home front. On his plantation south of town, B. L. C. Wailes had his servants dig up the floor of the smokehouse and boil the dirt to extract salt, and an old loom from the early 1800s was put back into operation to make cloth for uniforms.

Knowing that the situation was no better, and perhaps worse, throughout the South, ladies considered wearing out-of-style clothing and substituting items such as okra for coffee to be a badge of honor. In Vicksburg many did their part to raise funds for the boys in gray, giving entertainment for the Cause. One talented, Northern-born schoolmarm, Miss Mary Emma Hurlbut, gave a concert of patriotic songs, draped in a Confederate flag.

In February the inauguration of Jefferson Davis and Alexander Stephens as permanent president and vice-president was scheduled to be held in Richmond, following a general election (they had been serving under the provisional government). It was George Washington's birthday, which was also the time of the annual ball in Vicksburg, staged by Mollie Bunch's girls, who occupied a house of ill repute at the corner of Crawford and Mulberry. Everyone knew about the prostitutes' ball; most just

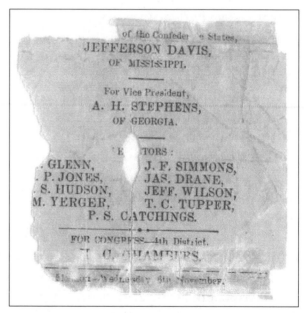

An original Confederate presidential ballot. (OCHM)

looked the other way, but this time, the girls went too far, over-stepping their bounds by sending invitations not only to their lovers but also to leading citizens and ministers.

On the evening of the ball, the fire bells rang as a mob of angry citizens took the engines to Madam Bunch's home on South Street, drenching the house and destroying furniture, then proceeding to the ball, where they turned the hoses on the dancers and also swept food from the banquet tables. From there, they went to a tavern operated by Pat Gorman and destroyed it. The episode ended with appearances in court, but no punishment was meted out, and no restitution was made.

The fracas had been only a brief diversion, for there were frightening dispatches in the newspapers that gave accounts of Northern troops, under the command of an obscure general named Ulysses S. Grant, capturing forts Henry and Donelson in Tennessee. The city's first real brush with war, however, occurred in early April, when the wounded from a place called Shiloh, over two hundred miles away, were brought to the city. With the arrival of each train, more men came, soon filling the hospitals to overflowing. Each facility was in dire need of help.

Answering the call were a group of women, under the leadership of Mrs. Elizabeth Eggleston, who organized the Ladies Hospital Association. With the hospitals, railroads, and private homes crowded with the wounded, Mahala Roach wrote in her diary, "It was a sad sight, and makes us realize that the war is near us indeed." City fathers realized it, too, as they set aside lots in Cedar Hill Cemetery for the burial of men who had made the ultimate sacrifice.

Just how near the war was came as a sudden shock a few weeks later when Adm. David G. Farragut's Union fleet, which had been patrolling the Gulf of Mexico south of New Orleans, made a move

A patriotic badge was advertised in the *Evening Citizen* in the spring of 1861. The emblem varied slightly for each state in the Confederacy. Shown is the version with the Palmetto Tree, representing South Carolina. (OCHM)

Gen. Martin Luther Smith was ordered to Vicksburg after the fall of New Orleans to take charge of the city's defenses. *(Battles and Leaders)*

against the two forts Jackson and St. Philip, which guarded the mouth of the Mississippi River. They defeated the Southern forces, then steamed upriver, landing troops and taking possession of the Crescent City.

Several days before the fall of New Orleans, Gen. P. G. T. Beauregard ordered Capt. D. B. Harris, chief engineer at Vicksburg, to plan fortifications for the city, specifically advising that the bluffs just north of town would be a good position and that there should also be a lower battery to defend the entrance to the Yazoo River. Beauregard warned that the enemy might try to dig a canal across the peninsula in front of the city, thus diverting the Mississippi River.

Col. James L. Autry had already been named military commander of Vicksburg, and he and Harris, with their troops and hundreds of slaves from nearby plantations, began the task of building fortifications.

News of the fall of New Orleans came on Saturday morning, April 26, 1862. The Louisiana city was only five days by river from Vicksburg, and there was little along the way to halt or even slow the Yankees' onslaught.

They were expected in Vicksburg in only a few days, and residents were bewildered and in disbelief at the rapid turn of events. Some chose to leave the city, seeking shelter with friends in the country, others camped in the woods far from the river, but many made up their minds to remain in town. Merchants closed their shops and packed their goods to be carted away to safety. On farms and plantations, cotton, stored in barns while planters anticipated the day when it could be sold, was burned on orders of the Confederate government, lest it be captured by the Yankees.

On May 12, Gen. Mansfield Lovell, who had been in command at New Orleans, ordered Gen. Martin L. Smith to Vicksburg.

When Smith arrived, displaced Confederate troops from South Louisiana were already in the city, and Smith found them, under the command of Autry, "pushing the works forward vigorously," laboring day and night, strengthening and building batteries and powder magazines, and mounting guns along the ridges. By the time the first enemy ships made their appearance, six of ten batteries had been completed and the cannoneers were at their posts.

The approach of the enemy was slower than expected. The bluecoats secured the surrender of Baton Rouge and then steamed to Natchez, where only one shot was fired before the town surrendered. South of Vicksburg, the towns of Grand Gulf and Warrenton were torched, and at Davis Bend, troops went ashore to burn the home of Joseph E. Davis. His brother Jefferson Davis fared better; they only ransacked his home, Brierfield.

On Sunday afternoon, May 18, several ships under the command of S. Phillips Lee dropped anchor before the city. Eventually, a small gig was lowered from the side of the *Oneida*, a white flag attached to its bow, and it made its way toward shore, to be met in midstream by a Confederate vessel. A message addressed to the "Authorities at Vicksburg" was handed to the Rebels. In the missive, Lee "demanded" the surrender of the city and said he expected a reply in three hours. Five hours passed before he received not one but three answers. Gen. Martin L. Smith tersely stated, "Having been ordered to hold these defenses, it is my intention to do so. . . ." Mayor Lazarus Lindsay advised that neither the city fathers or citizens would "ever consent to a surrender. . . ." If Lee doubted the messages, the reply of Col. James L. Autry, military governor of the post, should have left no doubt as to the course of action that lay ahead: "I have to state that Mississippians don't know, and refuse to learn how to surrender to an enemy. If

Col. James L. Autry thumbed his nose at the Yankees and dared them to try and take the city. (Mulvihill, *Vicksburg,* et al.)

21

Commodore Farragut or Brigadier General [Benjamin F.] Butler can teach them then let them come and try."

If the Yankees were expecting the same reaction in Vicksburg they had found in Natchez, they were sadly mistaken. Both cities had been Unionist strongholds, but each had sent her sons off to war, and battles and bloodshed had bonded them with the secessionists. When war came to their shores, there had been a change in the mood of Vicksburg residents, who chose defiance over complacent submission.

Vicksburg had thrown down the gauntlet not once but three times, and Farragut accepted the challenge; he would try to teach them how to surrender. The first shot was lobbed into the city on the afternoon of May 20, aimed at some Confederates on the bluff. Two days later, a fusillade was thrown against the fortifications, but there was no reply from the city's defenders. Smith explained later that as less than half the batteries had been completed, and guns at some had not yet been mounted, firing would have simply wasted ammunition. The silence, later broken by only sporadic firing, kept the enemy ignorant of Confederate strength, concealed the effects of their own shots, and kept the troops fresh and rested for a serious attack, which was expected.

From May 20 until mid-June, the Union guns fired at the town and at the troops' campsites. Then Farragut withdrew, dropping downriver only a few miles, anchoring out of range of the Rebel guns. His presence remained a lingering threat to the Southerners, who pondered his next move.

More troops were brought into the city, and more fortifications were constructed, while, from the north, Adm. David D. Porter's squadron approached after having captured Island No. 10 and Memphis.

To combine forces, Farragut would have to run the batteries.

Mississippians don't know, and refuse to learn how to surrender to an enemy.
—Col. James L. Autry

Opposite page: A rare Confederate print, engraved and printed in Columbia, South Carolina, depicts the Union bombardment of Vicksburg "On the ever memorable 28th of June, 1862." Prominent on the horizon to the left is the Warren County courthouse, which was a new building, and near the center is the spire of St. Paul Catholic Church. (OCHM)

[See page 24.]

| Monongahela. | Hartford. | Winona | Iroquois | Wissahicon. | Brooklyn. |

THE BOMBARDMENT OF THE CITY OF VICKSBURG.

On the ever memorable 28th of June 1862.

Lt. Isaac Newton Brown commanded the Confederate ironclad *Arkansas*. *(Battles and Leaders)*

His fleet again raised steam and appeared before the Vicksburg bluffs, where he unleashed his total strength, the guns of thirty-six warships bombarding the city for hours on June 28.

"The roar of the cannon was now continuous and deafening," Smith wrote. "Loud explosions shook the city to its foundations; shot and shell went hissing through the trees and walls, scattering fragments far and wide in the terrific flight; men, women and children rushed into the streets. . . ."

Later, under cover of darkness, the fleet began a stealthy move past the city. Suddenly, the Confederates opened fire, and a Southern soldier wrote, "The shells fell so fast that they looked like stars falling from the heavens. . . . the flashes of the cannon were that of lightning and its rumbling was that of thunder." Farragut had passed the batteries with little damage, though he had suffered 45 casualties to the South's 5. North of Vicksburg, Farragut and Porter were joined by Flag Officer Charles Davis, with four ironclads and six mortar scows, but to what avail? Early in the war, Lincoln had labeled Vicksburg's capture the key to victory, as it controlled the Mississippi. His forces now held all but four miles of the river, that which flowed in front of the Vicksburg batteries.

For sixty-seven days, almost three hundred cannons and mortars had rained an estimated 25,000 shot and shell into the city. The Confederates had held two powerful squadrons, accompanied by a land force of over four thousand men at bay. Not a Southern gun had been silenced or disabled, and the defenders had lost only 7 killed and 15 wounded.

The presence of the Yankees seemed to only stiffen the backbone of resistance. Farragut realized that he could do no more than temporarily silence the batteries and that the Confederates were capable of preventing his troops from landing, capturing, and holding the coveted prize. Porter agreed that it was a job for the army, not the navy. Before Farragut departed, however, he had a brush with the Confederacy's mysterious weapon, the ironclad CSS *Arkansas*.

There had been rumors for months about the proposed vessel being built at Yazoo City, some fifty miles above Vicksburg, but most seriously doubted the truth of the tales, and had they seen the pile of scrap metal and timbers from which the ship was crafted, few would have ever believed the mission could be accomplished. The rumors, however, persisted.

From atop the courthouse on July 15, 1862, Gens. Earl Van Dorn, John C. Breckinridge, and Stephen D. Lee watched as the vessel steamed down the Yazoo and into the Mississippi, small boats fleeing in front. Covered with railroad iron whose rust provided a natural camouflage, the *Arkansas* was equipped with rifled guns and a pointed bow capable of ramming any wooden ship. Catching the Union fleet off guard, she fought her way past them, inflicting serious damage, and also suffering some in return, before arriving at the safety of Vicksburg's docks, under the protection of Confederate batteries. Farragut was at first incredulous, then furious, that a crude Rebel ship had shamed the Union navy. After trying for a week to sink or destroy the *Arkansas* at her mooring, he abandoned the task, along with the hope of capturing Vicksburg, and, leaving Porter north of town, headed downstream on July 27.

In addition to the bombardments, Union forces had also undertaken a grandiose plan to divert the course of the Mississippi River (just as Beauregard had predicted) by digging a canal across the lower end of DeSoto Point, which would leave Vicksburg a city high and dry with no port. Gen. Thomas Williams used confiscated slaves to augment the troops who were handling the shovels, but numerous problems doomed the project. They, too, departed.

Lt. Dabney M. Scales made this sketch of the *Arkansas* while on board the vessel, which he dubbed the "Rebel Rascal." (OCHM)

[See page 31.]

EVEN AT HER MOORINGS, THE *ARKANSAS* WON IN A BATTLE WITH THE *ESSEX*

At four o'clock on the morning of the 22nd, I was awakened to the call to quarters, hurrying to our stations with not even a full compliment of men for 3 guns, our soldiers having just left the night before, we discovered the enemy coming right down upon us — We did not have a third of the firemen required in that department; consequently steam was behind hand. . . . we did not have enough to heave the anchor up and get under way, before the enemy got to us, even if we had had steam ready — So we had to lay in to the bank and couldn't meet him on anything like equal terms — His forces consisted of one large ironclad vessel mounting 8 more guns than we (18) and one ram protected by bales of compressed cotton all round — The gunboat was the Essex, the ram, I believe was the Queen of the West The Essex came first firing on us with her three bow guns — We replied with our two bow guns as long as they could be brought to bear — which was not a very long time, as our vessel being stationary, the enemy soon became too much on our broadside for these guns, and their crews had to be shifted to the broadside guns — In the meantime, the Essex ran up alongside us, and at that distance of 20 feet poured in a broads which crashed against our sides like nothing that I ever heard before — one 10 in. shot struck against the forward edge of one of the broadside ports which glanced in aft in a raking direction over the deck. This killed six of our men & wounded 4, leaving just two crews unhurt. We were so close that our men were burnt by the powder from the enemy's gun — We continued to fire our broadside and stern guns on the Essex, who had run astern of us, and it was now seen that she was unable to turn her head upstream and come alongside, as she evidently tried to do, but drifted down past the batteries to the lower fleet — All this time the Ram was not idle, but came close down on the heels of his consort — On he came, seeming bent on running us down. We welcomed him as warmly as we could with our scanty crew — Just before he got to us, we managed by the helm & with the aid of the starboard propellor, to turn our bow out stream a little, which prevented him from getting a fair lick at us — As it was, he glanced round our side, & ran aground just astern of us — This was the time we needed our men most; for had our stern

A photograph of Lt. Dabney Scales taken many years after the war. *(Confederate Veteran)*

guns (rifle 6 in.) been manned then, one could have blown her up or so disabled her as to have prevented her escape — But such was not the case, and the Ram succeeded in backing off very soon and "skedaddled" for her friends around the point. . . . We have since heard from the other side of the river, that six or eight of our shot penetrated the Essex killing and wounding a good many men — The Ram was struck 64 times by the Arkansas and the upper battery. . . .

—Lt. Dabney M. Scales, on board
the Confederate Steamer *Arkansas*
off Vicksburg, July 31, 1862

The *Essex*, a Union gunboat, tried but failed to sink the *Arkansas*. (OCHM)

Above: The *Arkansas*, with the *Capitol* alongside, is shown under construction in Yazoo City.

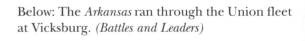

Below: The *Arkansas* ran through the Union fleet at Vicksburg. *(Battles and Leaders)*

Left: The *Arkansas* in the midst of battle *(Battles and Leaders)*
Below: With flag flying, the *Arkansas* was burned by her own crew near Baton Rouge to keep the ship from falling into Union hands. No enemy had ever set foot upon her deck. *(Harper's Weekly)*

"THE BRAVEST ACT . . ."

William Gilmore served as pilot of the *Arkansas*. (*Confederate Veteran*)

The bravest act I can recall was performed by a Louisville [Kentucky] man while on detached duty in the Confederate navy. William Gilmore was a pilot of the famous ram "Arkansas" when she ran the gauntlet of the Yankee fleet en route from Yazoo River to Vicksburg, on the 22nd of June, 1862. When just above the city Gilmore lost his bearings in the blinding smoke from the big guns, which were in full play on the enemy. The smoke stayed down on the water's surface, and he could see nothing from the little steel crib called "pilot house." He held the wheel as long as possible, but fearing he might take her to the bank, rang the stop bells, and instantly the vessel was almost at a standstill. He then went into the gun room, and while the forward gun at the starboard side was withdrawn to be recharged, he asked the chief gunner to wait a moment so that he could recover his bearings. Then the brave pilot leaped into the port hole to see the situation. Poor fellow! Just as he started to return to his wheel a shell from the enemy struck him in the middle of the head, completely carrying away the upper part of his body, and the lower limbs dropped back into the gun room limp. The shell crossed inside the vessel, striking point foremost on the breech of the forward gun on the starboard side, and, exploding, killed and maimed twenty-one other brave and true men. I was on the detail that buried the dead, and saw the "Arkansas" from the time she turned the point above. It was afterwards said that over one hundred thousand rounds were fired by the Yankees at the "Arkansas" and city of Vicksburg, and thirty-two thousand of them were sent inside of two hours. Old "Whistling Dick" got in some of his finest work that day, and the long line of water batteries we had above town never did better service.

—Tom Hall in
Confederate Veteran
May 1897

The Confederate First National Flag, with ten stars, was drawn by Miss Florence Lightcap in her autograph book. (OCHM)

The Union attack had failed, and Marmaduke Shannon could not help but gloat a bit on the pages of the *Whig:* "In the midst of all this, Vicksburg, proud, gallant little Vicksburg, firm as the eternal hills on which she reposes, gazes boldly and defiantly upon her enemy, and, with a feeling of inexpressible but justifiable pride she beholds two immense fleets. . . .unable to cope with her, compelled not only to keep a respectful distance, but, astounding as it may seem, actually forced to dig a new channel for the Mississippi! How humiliating to the United States. . . ."

Residents hoped for a return to a semblance of normalcy, but it was not to be. They had acted admirably during the two months of attacks, becoming accustomed to the dropping of the shells, going about their daily business. Often they watched the action from two of the city's best vantage points, a high plateau in the middle of town where the Genella family lived (called Sky Parlor Hill) or the cupola of the courthouse, which provided a view for many miles in any direction. Though Union shells had struck the Methodist church and numerous homes, there seemed to be little serious damage.

Some citizens had suffered minor privations, but a sense of patriotism usually prevailed. When Mahala Roach was told that a battery would have to be placed in her flower garden, she watched as shrubbery, fences, and walks were destroyed, stoically commenting, "I must bear my part of annoyance and trouble, as much as anyone else." She provided water for the thirsty soldiers, and when it rained (the Louisiana troops camped nearby had no tents), she put down pallets for them on her porches and in the house.

Casualties among the civilians were few. The *Whig* paid tribute to a widow, Mrs. Patience Gamble, who had been killed while trying to lead her little boy to safety. Editor Shannon wrote that she was

[See page 36.]

CANAL WAS FAILURE IN DIVERTING RIVER

His orders were to "cut off the neck of land beyond Vicksburg by means of a trench. . . .," and for four weeks in the summer of 1862, over a thousand slaves, taken from local plantations, worked with picks and shovels to divert the waters of the Mississippi River, hoping to change the course so that Union vessels could ply the stream without fear of Confederate guns on Vicksburg's bluffs.

The idea was conceived by Gen. Benjamin F. Butler, who ordered Gen. Thomas W. Williams to oversee the job. After three weeks, Williams reported "a temporary failure" and a week later abandoned the project.

"Williams' Ditch" became "Grant's Canal" in January 1863, when Gen. Henry W. Halleck revived the concept of changing the river channel. Grant put his men to work on the project, assuring Halleck that work was progressing as rapidly as possible. Lincoln suggested that the use of dredges would make it go even faster, and two were soon at the site.

There were also other similar projects underway. A canal at Duckport in Madison Parish, Louisiana, across the river from Vicksburg, was designed to connect the bayous that wound through the countryside, entering the Mississippi twenty miles south of the city, but low water forced the Yankees to abandon the project.

Upriver in Carroll Parish, troops began cutting a four-hundred-mile route from Lake Providence through the swamps, lakes, and bayous to a point below Vicksburg, but the work was halted when the Yazoo Pass expedition in the Mississippi Delta appeared more promising.

Meanwhile, work continued on Grant's Canal, though he reported in mid-February 1863 that the rise in the river had slowed his men's efforts.

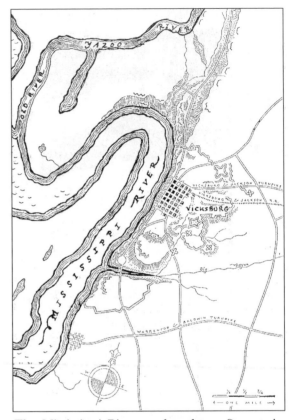

The Mississippi River made a large *S* curve in front of Vicksburg, and Union forces tried to cut a canal across the peninsula in front of the city. (OCHM)

Opposite page: Construction of the canal continued for months. (*The Soldier in Our Civil War*)

Adm. David D. Porter told Gen. William T. Sherman, whose men were among those endeavoring to complete the task, that "If this rain keeps up we won't need a canal. The whole peninsula will disappear, troops and all, in which case the gunboats will have the field to themselves."

Sherman thought "trying to turn the Mississippi by a ditch" was "a pure waste of human labor," and he wrote to Grant, "The river is about full and threatens to drown us out. The ground is wet, almost water, and it is impossible for wagons to haul stores from river to camp, or even for horses to wallow through. . . ." In addition to those problems, he said Confederate guns aimed at the mouth of the canal were playing havoc with the work.

In early March, Grant was still optimistic, writing that the job was nearly complete and "I will have Vicksburg this month, or fail in the attempt." By the end of the month, however, he reported that the Confederate cannoneers had "driven the dredges entirely out," and he had suspended all work.

Some of our men went over the river to where the Yanks were working at their canal — Williams Ditch, as they call it. They found about 600 Yankee graves, but worst of all they found about 500 negroes, most of them sick, and all left in the woods without anything to eat — or any provision whatever being made for them. They say they were worked hard in mud and water where their soldiers refused to work — And when they were taken sick, they were turned off to hunt a home, probably many miles distant — They were shot down like dogs, because they left the trench when we threw shells among them. This is the way the Yankees treat the race for whose freedom they pretend to fight.

—Dabney M. Scales
Confederate States navy
Written onboard the *Arkansas*
at Vicksburg, July 31, 1862

Slaves "freed" from local plantations by Union troops were put to work digging the canal. *(Harper's Weekly)*

REBEL CANNONEER DEVILED CANAL DIGGERS

My guns being of the largest caliber, and throwing shot and shell with equal effect, I was ordered to. . . .dispute the passage of any boats attempting to run the "canal". I. . . .found that two dredge boats had well-nigh succeeded in cutting through. I commenced, and kept up, both day and night, at regular intervals, a telling fire, and finally drove the dredge boats and batteries away, and put a quietus to all work on the "canal". . . . I could burst shell over and around them, just as well at night as in day, and the effect. . . .was a grand one. . . . Unless you have witnessed the transit and explosion of these huge missiles of death. . . . you can form no idea of its grandeur. As soon as it leaves the muzzle of the piece, you can see it, by aid of the burning fuse, shoot up, like a brilliant star, into mid-heaven, and trace it in its flight and descent until it explodes, when it throws out a sheet of flame and smoke. . . .The sight, I say, is a grand one, and the effect most terrible, as these immense shells break into fragments, go hissing through the air, and which, in their fall, are as deadly as solid shot. . . .

—Capt. William Capers
Company G, 1st Louisiana Heavy Artillery
Stationed south of Vicksburg

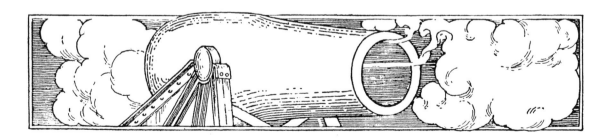

struck "by a bloody messenger of tyranny." She was Vicksburg's first civilian casualty.

Slowly business was resumed, and though luxury items were available, the costs were exorbitant. Salt could not even be bought for $100 a sack, and butter sold for $1.50 a pound. Whiskey had gone up $20 a gallon in one day, from $40 to $60. With an army camped near the city and officers bringing their families to Vicksburg, the problems of food and shelter were compounded. Talk always seemed to center on war and food.

There was, perhaps, a cautious sense of relief that the enemy had departed, but always there were the Yankees upriver, just in sight, maneuvering and occasionally firing a volley, an unnerving reminder that the city was safe only, as a Confederate soldier wrote, "until the Yankeys pay us another visit." The ladies of Vicksburg called on a higher authority than the government, seeking a day of humiliation, fasting, and prayer, "that we may once more live free from the Cares and Foes that beset us. . . ."

A military reorganization soon placed a new officer in charge of the Vicksburg defenses. The president named John C. Pemberton, who was promoted to lieutenant general on October 13, 1862, as commander of the Department of Mississippi and East Louisiana, replacing Gen. Earl Van Dorn, who had assumed duties on the day before the all-out assault the previous June. On July 4, Van Dorn had declared martial law in several coastal and river cities, including Vicksburg, an order that prompted violent protests from the public. Van Dorn rescinded the order two months later. He would serve as commander of cavalry under Pemberton, whose headquarters were at Grenada.

There were rumors that Gen. William T. Sherman and his army planned to advance on Vicksburg from the north, and as fall came to a close and winter began to make its first blustery appearance,

Patience Gamble's death was reported in the *Whig*. She was the first Vicksburg civilian to lose her life in the war.

Admiral Porter assembled a flotilla at the mouth of the Yazoo River, with the purpose of destroying Confederate batteries and setting up landing areas for the army.

Porter was in for a surprise. For some months, Confederates had been experimenting with an electrically activated torpedo or mine. A team of engineers and scientists took glass demijohns and affixed them to floats that would suspend the apparatus just below the surface of the water. Strategically anchored in the channel of the Yazoo, copper wires were extended to hideouts on shore, where volunteers stood by to secretly detonate the mines at the right moment.

On December 12, 1862, a Federal squadron of five vessels steamed up the river. Suddenly, there was an explosion, then another. The ironclad USS *Cairo* had become the first victim, settling to the bottom in thirty-six feet of water in about twelve minutes. The Confederates had made naval history—never before had a ship been sunk by a mine.

Along with the news of the sinking of the enemy ship, local morale was bolstered by a visit from President Davis, accompanied by Gen. Joseph E. Johnston. For two days, they inspected the defenses, from Snyder's Bluff north of town to Warrenton below. They also met with Pemberton, whose name would forever be linked to Vicksburg within the coming year. It was the first time Davis had come home since the grand send-off for him on his way to Montgomery almost two years earlier.

Though Christmas arrived cold, rainy, and bleak, it was a time of gaiety at the Crawford Street home of Dr. and Mrs. William T. Balfour, who entertained the Confederate officers and their friends. The music was interrupted late in the night as an anxious, mud-spattered courier made his way through the dancers to give Gen. Martin L. Smith the news that eighty-one vessels—gunboats

A sketch depicts the demijohn and explosives used to sink the *Cairo*. (Mulvihill, *Vicksburg*, et al.)

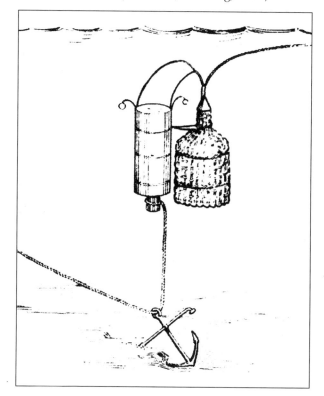

and transports—had passed Lake Providence, Louisiana, headed for Vicksburg. The party broke up abruptly as Smith excitedly told the guests, "This ball is at an end; the enemy is coming down the river. . . ."

The rumor that Sherman was coming was now a reality. He planned to land north of town, attack the fortifications along the bluffs, then turn south to take the city. Sherman's maps showed Chickasaw Bayou meandering for a mile in front of the bluffs before draining a five-mile plain into the Yazoo. What the map did not show was the forbidding nature of the terrain, for the low land was a mixture of open wooded areas and sloughs. In addition, Confederates had felled trees to further slow the enemy.

Sherman's 32,000 men found themselves in a tangle of downed trees and water up to their waists in a dismal swamp. Facing them were only 6,000 Rebels, but they were on top of the bluffs. Not only was geography the enemy but also the elements, for a cold, driving rain set in for days.

Confederates opened fire, the cannons belching a constant stream of iron and lead, a hail of bullets pushing the Yankees back. Some of them, who had made it through the mud and muck, found themselves at the base of the bluffs where the Southerners literally leaned over the edge, firing down, swatting them like flies. The trapped men desperately tried to dig shelters in the embankment with their hands.

The attack had failed, and Sherman's men, shivering in the cold, driving rain, awaited orders to renew the assault. Sherman, however, was working out a plan with Porter to move 10,000 troops up the river to Dromgould's Bluff and outflank the Rebels. A dense fog, however, stalled any action. The rain continued to pour, and Porter wrote that the winter wind "howled like a legion of devils." The next night, the skies were clear, but the moon was

Ripped open by Confederate mines, the U.S.S. Cairo *sank quickly to the bottom of the Yazoo.*

[See page 44.]

Above: The ironclad U.S.S. *Cairo,* one of Ead's City Class Gunboats, was sunk in the Yazoo River on December 12, 1862. It was the first boat ever sunk by a mine (then called a torpedo). Salvaged 102 years later, it is on display in the Vicksburg National Military Park.

Left: The fuse wire used in detonating the mine that sank the *Cairo* is on display in the Old Court House Museum. (OCHM by C. Todd Sherman)

Right: Confederates pull survivors aboard a yawl in the Mississippi River at Vicksburg in 1863 after the Union tug *Sturges* was destroyed by the Confederate river batteries. (Browne, *Four Years in Secessia*)

Left: Union soldiers, escaping from a burning ship, were captured and jailed by the Confederates. (Richardson, *The Secret Service*)

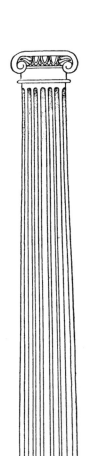

APPROACH OF ENEMY BOATS ENDED BALFOUR BALL

"I hears a boat coming," an excited little black girl told the two Confederate officers who sat in their shanty on Christmas Eve 1862, playing cards. "Marse Ainhart, you and Marse Daniel better come out here."

"Come now," replied Maj. E. P. Earnheart, "you are dreaming, Artie."

"No sah! I hears it say choo, choo, pat, pat, pat," the excited child replied, illustrating the chug of the steam engines and the slapping of the paddle wheel against the water.

Earnheart and Maj. Lee L. Daniels walked to the porch of their little building, which was located on Horace Tibbots' plantation, about eleven miles south of Lake Providence, Louisiana, and listened intently. The sounds Artie had described were barely audible, and the two men headed for the riverbank an eighth of a mile away, where they waited perhaps thirty minutes.

They could hear the sound getting closer and closer, and eventually, "a monster turned the bend, two miles above us, and came slowly as if feeling the way," Daniels wrote in 1904 in an account to Gen. Stephen D. Lee. Then Earnheart whispered, "Here comes another."

Some sparks flew out of Major Earnheart's pipe, and Daniels grabbed the pipe and put out the fire, warning that those boats would fire a volley at the crack of a match. Soon, the "large black devil was abreast of us, in easy gun shot from our double barrels, but suicide to fire. We counted, counted, counted in all seven gunboats, fifty-nine transports loaded with blue coats," Daniels continued.

The night was cloudy, cold, and drizzly, so the two men waited

An invitation to a ball at the Balfour House is from the Old Court House Museum Collection. (OCHM)

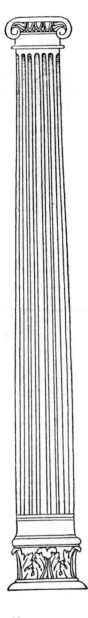

until they were sure no more boats were in the flotilla, and then Daniels, who had been a telegraph operator in Vicksburg before the war began, jumped onto his little bay filly and practically flew to the telegraph offices, some three miles back in the woods, where he sent a message to the other end of the line.

Daniels was frantic; he knew that if he didn't get the message through that unsuspecting Vicksburg would fall to the enemy. It was a little past midnight, and it only took twenty-seven seconds to transmit the words, although to Daniels it seemed that his friend on the other end of the line would never answer.

Col. Philip H. Fall, also from Vicksburg, was on duty at the little telegraph office on DeSoto Point, across the river from Vicksburg, when the message came through.

"Golly, old fellow, what's up?" Fall answered when he got the first signal.

Almost half a century later, Daniels recalled this message, which he said was indelible in his brain after all those years: "Great God, Phil, where have you been? I have been calling (I am afraid I said half an hour instead of half a minute) and the river is lined with boats, almost a hundred have passed my lookout. Seven gunboats and fifty-nine transports chock full of men. God speed you, rush across and give the alarm."

Philip Fall tapped a reply: "God bless you, Lee, bye, bye, we may never meet again."

Almost immediately, Colonel Fall was in a small skiff, headed across the Mississippi to Vicksburg. It was a tempestuous night, and at times, it appeared the waves of the river would extinguish the colonel's red lantern, which signaled the men at the batteries along the bluffs that he was friend not foe.

Had the light gone out, Fall might have been annihilated. Despite the possibility of death, he was determined to make the

Lee Daniels, posing for this photo many years after the war, sent the telegram to Gen. M. L. Smith at the Balfour ball. Daniels also personally took a telegram to Jefferson Davis in 1861, advising him that he had been elected president of the Confederate States. (*Confederate Veteran*)

crossing, for the city was in peril. Had the message not been sent when it was, the city probably would have been taken, for only a short time later, the telegraph wires were cut by the enemy.

Within half an hour, after he had received the message, Col. Philip H. Fall was at the Balfour House on Crawford Street where Dr. and Mrs. William T. Balfour were entertaining the officers and their ladies at a Christmas ball. The house was ablaze with lights, and the sounds of music filled the cold night air.

Suddenly, the door burst open, and a gray-clad courier, muddy and disheveled, made his way through the dancers (who gave him a wide berth) and stopped in front of Gen. Martin Luther Smith, Confederate commander of Vicksburg. General Smith scanned the courier critically and, frowning, asked, "Well, sir, what do you want?"

Colonel Fall replied that a flotilla of gunboats and transports had passed Lake Providence, headed downriver. General Smith turned pale and, in a loud voice, exclaimed, "THIS BALL IS AT AN END; THE ENEMY IS COMING DOWN RIVER; ALL NON-COMBATANTS MUST LEAVE THE CITY." Then the shocked general turned to Colonel Fall and thanked him for the message and apologized for his harsh manner. Immediately, men reported to their stations; by the end of the week, the Battle of Chickasaw Bayou was history.

The story might have ended differently had not a little slave girl first sounded the alarm that broke up the Balfour ball.

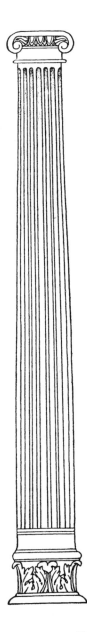

*This ball
is at an end . . .*

so bright that a surprise move was impossible. In addition, Grant, who was to have moved down from North Mississippi by land from Holly Springs, had not been able to keep his part of the bargain as Van Dorn's cavalry had destroyed his supply depot.

Learning that the new commander at Vicksburg, General Pemberton, had reinforced the ranks of the Confederates, a disheartened Sherman loaded his men on their transports and headed upriver on January 2, 1863. He had suffered a loss of 1,779 to the Confederates 187. His report had a sullen tone: "I reached Vicksburg at the time appointed, landed, assaulted, and failed."

The old year ended, and the new one began with a decidedly Confederate victory. It was Sherman's first independent command in the field, and at Chickasaw Bayou, Southerners had taught him that indeed war was hell.

Chickasaw Bayou, where Sherman was soundly defeated (*Review of Reviews*)

I reached Vicksburg at the time appointed, landed, assaulted, and failed.

—Gen. William T. Sherman

Gen. Stephen D. Lee

Chickasaw Bayou and the bluffs beyond, which Yankee troops tried to scale *(Battles and Leaders)*

Their orders were to burn the Vicksburg.

Their orders were to burn the vessel, and when the task was completed, each of the soldiers who helped was given a ninety-day furlough for "Gallant and meritorious conduct. . . ." They had not only performed their duty, but they had also done so under the threat of enemy guns on the Yankee ships *Hartford* and *Albatross*.

Vicksburg, a Confederate transport, had been tied up at the city waterfront when she was rammed on the night of February 2, 1863, by the *Queen of the West*. Adm. David D. Porter reported to Secretary of the Navy Gideon Wells that the Union guns had set her on fire and left her in a sinking condition. The Confederates, however, had put out the fire and kept the boat afloat with pumps, buying time so they could strip her of her engine and other useful materials.

During the night of March 28, 1863, a spring storm hit the city, and the shell of the ship broke loose and drifted downriver, the wind driving it aground at John Henderson's plantation below Warrenton. It was easy prey for the enemy, so the decision was made to destroy it. Marmaduke Shannon, editor of the *Vicksburg Daily Whig*, reported on April 1 that "an expedition was gotten up . . . and the glare of the pallid light, that in fearful grandeur was dispelling the wild darkness of night in the neighborhood of Diamond Bend early on yesterday morning, indicated that our brave lads were successful. She had been set on fire, and in a short time burned to the water's edge. . . ."

Shannon speculated that the Yankees had dreamed of the glory of destroying the *Vicksburg*, but the Confederates had denied them of that privilege. The editor noted that the machinery had been sent to Selma, Alabama, and that the boat's "bright days were long since gone and she could have only been used as a wharfboat hereafter."

The only mention by the Confederates in the *Official Records* was a report by Gen. Carter L. Stevenson that "The *Vicksburg* burned." Special Order No. 95, however, issued and signed by Gen. John C. Pemberton, expressed appreciation and told of the bravery of the men.

A copy of the order, commending Pvt. Benjamin Williams Ellison of Company C, 3rd Tennessee Infantry, one of the men who destroyed the *Vicksburg,* is owned by his descendant, David Reid of Broken Bow, Oklahoma.

The *Queen of the West* rammed the *Vicksburg* on the night of February 2, 1863. *(Harper's Weekly)*

With Charley Edwards holding on for dear life, the hog raced toward the bluff as the men tried to turn or stop the animal.

It was the summer of 1862, with little happening to occupy the time of Col. Tom Hunt's Kentuckians, who were sent to keep Farragut's ships from landing at the Vicksburg waterfront. The men had turned to the ridiculous to kill time, organizing a race between two wild hogs, ridden by two men of the company.

As their comrades cheered, the two riders held onto the hogs' ears as the race began. The Yankees heard the excited shouts and turned their guns toward the Confederates to dampen their spirits. One shell burst close enough to spatter them with dirt, hurting no one, but the pigs were so badly scared that they panicked and bolted. One threw his rider, but young Charley Edwards, a raw recruit only in service for three months, held onto his noble steed. The hog and Charley both went over the cliff, the hog surviving but the man breaking his back and dying within moments.

One of the men wrote that it cast gloom over the camp, but that night, as a measure of revenge, they dined on pork, having slaughtered the hapless hog.

—William C. Davis in
The Orphan Brigade

A Confederate vessel with a load of cattle steams upriver toward Vicksburg. *(Harper's Weekly)*

Refugees from Vicksburg hid or camped in the woods outside the city during the bombardment in 1862, and some fled before the siege began in 1863. This scene by an English artist shows camp activities, such as maids attending the children while a lady reads a dispatch just brought by a soldier on horseback. (*The Illustrated London News,* August 20, 1863)

THE DAILY CITIZEN.

J. M. SWORDS,........Proprietor

VICKSBURG, MISS.

THURSDAY, JULY 2, 1863.

☞ Mrs. Cisco was instantly killed on Monday, on Jackson road. Mrs. Cisco's husband is now in Virginia, a member of Moody's artillery, and the death of such a loving, affectionate and dutiful wife will be a loss to him irreparable.

☞ We are indebted to Mr. G'l.......... a steak of Confederate beef alias m......... have tried it, and can assure our friend...... it is rendered necessary, they need h........ scruples at eating the meat. It is sweet,..... and tender, and so long as we have a.......... left we are satisfied our soldiers will be con....... to subsist on it.

☞ Jerre Askew, one of our most esteem...... merchant-citizens, was wounded at the wor..... in the rear of our city a few days since, an...... breathed his last on Monday. Mr. Askew wa...... a young man of strict integrity, great industry...... and an honor to his family and friends. H...... was a member of Cowan's artillery, and by th...... strict discharge of his duties and his obliging...... disposition, won the confidence and esteem of...... his entire command. May the blow his family...... have sustained be mitigated by Him who doeth...... all things well.

☞ Grant's forces did a little firing on Tuesday afternoon, but the balance of that day was comparatively quiet. Yesterday morning they were very still, and continued so until early in the afternoon, when they sprung a...... mine on the left of our centre, a...... along the line f........................ city been s... ....molasses at ten dollars per gallon....... corn at ten dollars per bushel! We have not as yet proved the fact upon the parties accused, but this allusion to the subject may induce some of our citizens to ascertain

GOOD NEWS.—In devoting a large portion of our space this morning to Federal intelligence, copied from the Memphis Bulletin of the 25th it should be remembered that the news, in the original truth, is whitewashed by the Federal Provost Marshal, who desires to hood wink the poor Northern white slaves. The former editors of the Bulletin being rather pro-southern men, were arrested for speaking the truth when truth was unwelcome to Yankerdom........... in the chain-gang workin................ where they now are................................ da................ resa..................................

.... the ....people.. ure, morti- tying as i................ope that a salutary improvem.............. matters will be made b.......t military authorities.

ON DIT.—That the great Ulysses—the Yankee Generalissimo, surnamed Grant—has expressed his intention of dining in Vicksburg on Saturday next, and celebrating the 4th of

Yankee News From All Points.

PHILADELPHIA, June 21, 2 30 A. M.—The following is all the news of interest in the Washington Star:

Major Brazill, of the United States volunteers, received intelligence from Fayette county, Penn., this morning that the rebels in heavy force were advancing on Pittsburg via the National road leading from Cumberland across the Alleghany Mountains. Their pickets had reached Grantsville, Md., thirty-eight miles from Uniontown, Fayette county, Penn., on Wednesday evening last.

It is reported in Washington to-day that two members of Hooker's staff were gobbled up by guerillas last night in the vicinity of Fairfax.

HARRISBURG, June 20.—Operations were commenced on our side to-day by a portion of a New York cavalry regiment, capturing twenty rebel prisoners at McConnelsburg, in Fulton county.

Col. Lawrence, with a portion of the 127th Pennsylvania regiment, (mounted) captured a squad of rebels who were marauding on this side of the river.

We hold Chambersburg and the citizens are arming and fortifying the city. Gen. Couch had ordered that the place be held.

The Fortifications opposite this city are ...hed, and are considered impregnable ...he rebels are known to be 8000 stron... ...erstown and Williamsport. ...e rebels in the north ...iver, from Cumber' ...Gen. K.......... ...as may ...nd wo.D.n................carried him if ...od.murals'..............ceived a dispatc... ...Tue.................g that Junkins had ...o...................and had thrown ou... ...side, but withdrew them ...re is no information at ...bel infantry at Hagerstown. ...been plundering horses in the ...General Couch received a dis... ...t confirming the report of rebel ...tysburg.

...June 21, 8 P M.—Latest advices ...4, say that heavy firing wa... ...heard there at intervals throughout the day.

BALTIMORE, June 21.—The rebels made their appearance at Frederick yesterday evening and about 7 o'clock a body of cavalry reached Monocacy bridge, four miles this side of Frederick. The rebels paroled all the sick in the hospital and every Government employe. They searched the stables for horses, seizing all marked U. S. A very large force of rebel infantry, cavalry and artillery crossed at Antietam during yesterday. Refugees say they number from 40,000 to 50,000, but pickets report them at 25,000. Earthworks are

...remity in the city. These were celebrated by Union League men, who are being armed by Gen. Schenck. The Union men are confident that the rebels will not be so rash as to attempt a raid in that direction. The disloyal among us are evidently uneasy, and begin to realize that any hostile movement of the rebel army against Baltimore might result disastrously among themselves.

A Herald's special from Monocacy Station, Md., the 21st, says: About 4 o'clock P M. Major Cole, of the 1st Maryland cavalry, made a gallant dash into Frederick, was forty minutes driving out the enemy, killing two and capturing one. No loss on our side. Our cavalry passed through the city, and immediately after about 1500 rebel cavalry re-occupied the town.

Rebel cavalry entered Frederick yesterday. P. M., about 6 o'clock, and dashed furiously through the city, capturing nine of our men on duty at the signal station, and paroled invalid soldiers, numbering about six v. hospital. A number of horses Secession flags were displayed Hotel, and some citizens ...rant welcome the rebels. ulation evinced t...... ladies were exce............de our city are con- demonstrati................ ...g sick list. Fever, dysentry of sympt...............s are their companions, and Grant ....ngir master. The boys are deserting daily ....d are crossing the river in the region of Warrenton, cursing Grant and abolitionists generally. The boys are down upon the earth delving the burrowing, the bad water, and the hot weather.

GONE OUT.—The National Intelligencer of Washington has closed its long career in a suspension and a sale of its effects at auction.— It has been highly respectable and very mischievous in its day and generation. An old union prop falls with it. If we had the writing of its epitaph we should say, "Old Grimes is dead"

NOTE.

JULY 4th. 1863.

Two days bring about great changes, The banner of the Union floats over Vicksburg. Gen. Grant has "caught the rabbit;" he has dined in Vicksburg, and he did bring his dinner with him. The "Citizen" lives to see it. For the last time it appears on "Wall-paper." No more will it eulogize the luxury of mule-meat and fricassed kitten—urge Southern war

Lt. Gen. John C. Pemberton, a Pennsylvanian, was commander of the Confederate troops at Vicksburg. His portrait is imposed over a copy of the newspaper printed on wallpaper during the siege. (OCHM)

THE 1863 CAMPAIGN FOR VICKSBURG

*We are encampt within full view of the
Much coveted city of Vicksburg the
Taking of which will cost the lives of
Many a brave and true soldier.*

—Matthew R. Adams
Company B, 13th Illinois Infantry
January 31, 1863

The Union defeat at Chickasaw Bayou marked the end of the 1862 campaign for Vicksburg, and the Rebels had clearly won a great victory. Such a terrible loss of life for no gain might have shaken a lesser man, but for someone with Ulysses S. Grant's tenacity, the next step was obvious: "There was nothing left to be done but to go forward to a decisive victory," he recalled.

The major problem confronting Grant as he planned his new campaign was how to approach the Hill City. The obvious answer was to pull back to Memphis, regroup, and then begin another overland campaign following the path of the Mississippi Central Railroad. Grant was quick to reject this option, as it would have the appearance to the Northern public of being a retreat in the wake of a defeat.

Having rejected the overland route, Grant settled on another option: "To secure a footing upon dry ground on the east side of the river from which troops could operate against Vicksburg." Toward this end, Grant began shifting his troops from Memphis to join Sherman's, who were already encamped opposite Vicksburg

II.

The Next Gale
from the North
Will Bring to
Our Ears

The Clash of Resounding Arms

—Patrick Henry, March 23, 1775,
in his speech before the
Virginia Convention

51

on the Louisiana side of the river. By the end of January 1863, most of the Army of the Tennessee was with Sherman. The Army of the Tennessee at this time consisted of four corps: the 13th, commanded by Gen. John A. McClernand; the 15th, commanded by Gen. William T. Sherman; the 17th, commanded by Gen. James B. McPherson; and the 16th, commanded by Gen. Stephen A. Hurlbut. The 16th Corps remained in Western Tennessee and had only a supporting role in the campaign, so all told, Grant had some 44,000 troops to begin his operations against Vicksburg.

With the decision made to move on Vicksburg from the river, Grant needed a workable plan to make this goal a reality. Planning an amphibious assault into hostile territory took time, and the last thing that Grant wanted was for his troops to lie idle all winter while the details of the assault were worked out. Thus, he began a series of experiments to keep his troops active and possibly have the added benefit of finding a water route his troop transports could use to land men in the Mississippi without having to run them past the Vicksburg river batteries.

The Federals carried out four separate expeditions trying to find a safe water route around Vicksburg: the Duckport Canal, Lake Providence, Yazoo Pass, and Steele's Bayou. Despite great efforts, none of these expeditions succeeded. Grant, however, was not concerned: he later stated, "All these failures would have been very discouraging if I had expected much from the efforts; but I had not."

The expeditions to find a safe route around Vicksburg had ended in failure, but in the meantime, Grant decided on a plan for taking Vicksburg. He was going to march his troops down the Louisiana side of the river to a point below Vicksburg, then use transports to ferry his men across to Mississippi. Once the beachhead was secure, Grant would move inland and operate against Vicksburg.

MAJ. GEN. U. S. GRANT.

Entered according to Act of Congress, A. D. 1863, by BARR & YOUNG, in the Clerk's Office of the District Court of the U. S. for the So. District of Ohio.

Following his victory, General Grant posed for this photograph in Vicksburg by army photographers Barr & Young. (OCHM)

Grant realized that for his operation to be a success, he had to have the cooperation of the United States Navy to protect his troop transports during the actual landing. Accordingly, one of the first people Grant told of his plan was Rear Adm. David Dixon Porter, commander of the Union fleet anchored above Vicksburg.

Porter was quick to offer his support to Grant, and on the night of April 16, 1863, he ran seven ironclads, one armored ram, three transports, and one tug past the Vicksburg river batteries. The passage was a great success with only one transport, the *Henry Clay*, being destroyed by Confederate fire. On April 22, six more transports successfully passed the defenses, the only losses being one ship sunk and one damaged.

On March 29, 1863, Grant put his army into motion by ordering Gen. John McClernand to march his 13th Army Corps from their camps at Milliken's Bend above Vicksburg on the Louisiana side of the river to New Carthage, twenty-seven miles to the south. From New Carthage, McClernand moved his corps to Hard Times, Louisiana, just across the river from Grand Gulf, Mississippi, where the landing was scheduled to take place. McClernand's men were loaded aboard the transports on April 29, and with their protective escort of seven gunboats, the ships steamed toward Grand Gulf.

The town of Grand Gulf was defended by Confederate general John S. Bowen, who had under his command approximately 8,000 men. To protect the Mississippi as it flowed in front of the town, the Confederates had built forts Cobun and Wade, both of which mounted heavy guns to sweep the river. Before the defenseless transports could land, these guns had to be silenced by the U.S. Navy's ironclads.

While the transports waited in the middle of the river, safely out of range of the Confederate batteries, the gunboats closed with

Gen. John S. Bowen commanded the Confederate troops at the Battle of Port Gibson. *(Battles and Leaders)*

53

the forts and opened fire. The Confederates quickly responded, and the air was soon filled with shot and shell. One witness to the bombardment was George Smith of Company H, 33rd Illinois Infantry. The young lieutenant was awed by the power of the bombardment and said of it, "The Gun Boats were in line in front of the bluff & poured in fire that was awful to behold. The whole cliff blazed with the flash of guns & the water splashed & boiled & foamed, with the shower of plunging hissing shot. They seemed alive with all things that hiss & howl & scream."

The Union bombardment went on for hours, but the navy was unable to silence the Confederate guns, and the landing had to be called off, as the unarmored transports were easy targets for the Rebel cannoneers. Undaunted by his repulse on the twenty-ninth, Grant loaded his men back on the transports April 30 and moved his forces south of Grand Gulf to Bruinsburg, Mississippi, where he landed with no opposition. Grant later said of the accomplishment, "all the campaigns, labors, hardships, and exposures from the month of December previous to this time that had been made and endured were for the accomplishment of this one object."

With Grant now on Mississippi soil, Bowen at Grand Gulf quickly moved most of his army to Port Gibson to block the Federal army's move inland. The Rebel general was at a severe disadvantage, however, as he had only 8,000 men with which to try and stop Grant's 23,000. Bowen was outnumbered because several diversions by Grant kept adequate reinforcements from being sent to the Confederate commander.

The first diversion was a cavalry raid through the heart of Mississippi, led by Gen. Benjamin Grierson. Riding out of La Grange, Tennessee, on April 17, Grierson pushed his 1,700 men south, destroying railroad tracks and anything else of military

Sgt. Seth Enos Hall
Company F, 8th Iowa Infantry
(OCHM)

I have seen 40 or 50 plantation dwellings burned in the last 2 days . . .
—Seth Enos Hall, May 8, 1863

value. The Federals pushed on through Mississippi, finally reaching the safety of Union-held Baton Rouge on May 2.

The second diversion began on April 30, when General Sherman loaded a division of his men on transports and, with three gunboats as escorts, steamed up the Yazoo River and acted as though he intended to assault the Confederates at Snyder's Bluff, just north of Vicksburg. The ironclad escorts pounded the Rebel defenses on April 30 and May 1 as Grant was making his crossing of the Mississippi. At the end of the second day of fighting, Sherman pulled his troops out and began moving south to catch up with Grant and the rest of the army.

Grant's diversions worked perfectly on Gen. John C. Pemberton—the attacks were a major distraction and left him unsure of where the main Federal attack would come; thus he failed to heed Bowen's warnings that the Yankees were massing at Hard Times and did not send Bowen the large numbers of men he so desperately needed.

Bowen deployed his force five miles west of Port Gibson to block Grant's movement into the interior of the state. Although he was outnumbered, Bowen did have one advantage, as the terrain was highly suited for a defensive fight. The area west of Port Gibson was cut by deep depressions that were filled with thick undergrowth and canebrakes. The main routes through the area, the Rodney and Bruinsburg roads, ran along the tops of the ravines, and once off the roads and deployed for battle in the vine-choked ravines, keeping control of an attacking army would be very difficult.

The Federal column pressing inland ran into the Confederates about midnight on May 1, 1863, and a brisk skirmish broke out. With the coming of dawn, the fighting grew in intensity as the Federals pressed the attack. In the early afternoon, Bowen wired Pemberton, "We have been engaged in a furious battle ever since

*The Gun Boats . . .
poured in fire
that was awful
to behold.*

daylight; losses very heavy. The men act nobly, but the odds are overpowering."

Bowen was correct in his assessment of the situation—his men had fought very bravely, but the superior Federal numbers turned the tide in favor of the attackers, and by five thirty in the evening, the general had to withdraw his troops from the battlefield to avoid being cut off and surrounded. The battle had been a very fierce one, and the losses reflected this: the Confederates had 1,327 casualties and the Federals 875.

After his defeat at Port Gibson, Bowen marched his command to the north side of the Big Black River and to safety. The Grand Gulf defenses were abandoned and soon occupied by the Federals to use as a supply dump for Grant's army. Before continuing his advance, Grant waited a week to build up his supplies and allow Sherman to catch up to the army with his corps. Most of Sherman's men had arrived by the evening of May 7, and the next day, Grant gave the order for his blue columns to march.

The Federal troops who marched out of Port Gibson moved off to the northeast instead of heading due north for Vicksburg. This was in accordance with Grant's plan: he wanted to move to the northeast and sever the Southern Railroad somewhere near Edwards. This would cut off the Vicksburg garrison from supplies and reinforcements being sent through Jackson. Then Grant would turn his army west and march directly on the city.

In the march toward the Southern Railroad, McClernand's corps was the left of the Union army, Sherman's corps the center, and McPherson's corps the right. Pemberton had his forces carefully guarding the Big Black River crossings, watching for Grant to move directly on Vicksburg. Pemberton was in no rush to confront Grant, as he was still awaiting reinforcements from South Carolina and Port Hudson, Louisiana.

Vicksburg residents and Confederate troops expected Gen. Joseph E. Johnston (above), commanding troops near Jackson, to come to their aid, but he never came. (OCHM)

[See page 61.]

CHURCH WAS HIT BY SHELLS

A large parrott shell, fired by a Union gun on DeSoto Point, across the river from Vicksburg, crashed through one window, zoomed across the sanctuary of St. Paul Catholic Church, and out another window on June 28, 1863, as Rev. John B. Bannon, Confederate chaplain with the Missouri troops, was saying mass.

Some felt it was not a stray shot, and Louisiana soldier and journalist Will Tunnard wrote that when the enemy saw a large number of people congregated on the steps of the church they "instantly opened on them with a Parrott gun. As the shells came screaming wickedly through the streets, exploding or entering the building, men, women and children hastily sought shelter to escape the danger. . . . Such an unheard of, ruthless and barbarous method of warfare as training a battery of rifled cannon upon an assembly of unarmed men and worshipping women is unparalleled in the annals of history."

One Southern soldier, sufficiently recovered from his wounds to attend services, wrote that all the women fled the building, but Father Bannon, used to taking risks in performing his regular duties, continued mass as if nothing had happened, but when he turned to his audience, he found the church was practically empty.

An 1863 photo inscribed "From Court House Dome" shows St. Paul Catholic Church (with steeple), the Baptist church to the left (its steeple had been destroyed by the shelling), and Sky Parlor Hill in the background between the two. (OCHM)

UNION PRISONER FOUND JAIL UNCLEAN

".... we had to surrender. They took our guns what were not thrown away and marched us for Vicksburg leading us through a swamp of water knee deep. After getting inside of their Breastworks they did not take us in a straight direction to the City but marched us several miles out of our way reaching Pembertons Headquarters at midnight and they kept us there until morning because he did not want to be disturbed we started soon as daylight and marched to the jail about one half mile distant on the same street they put us into the jail yard and then most of our escort left us with the exception of a guard around the jail yard wall We found our new quarters full as comfortable as we expected although very unclean and filled with vermin The jail was a good sized two story building very strongly built & composed of Brick a small cook house of the same material filled one corner of the yard and from this important institution twice a day they gave us a piece of cornbread and a small piece of Indian Rubber Beef and what they call coffee could be made from the bran of the meal a few Negroes performed the cooking opperation. They paroled us the first day and told us we were to be sent across the River into our lines on the following morning and we were looking forward all day Hopefull to when the time should arrive. Our men kept up an almost incessant fire from our Mortar boats and almost every shell passed over or alighted near us three of them burst in the yard during our stay most fortunately harming no one when it came night we could see them quite plainly and their terrible whistling and Howling gave us no rest for half the night. Morning came bringing with it disapointment for instead of sending us across the river as they said they told us we could not go then and they did not know when we could. It seemed as though they wished to keep us so as to have us exposed to our mens fire all they could but along near night one of their officers (Major Watts) who came to make some inquiries of one of the crew of the Cincinati told us we should go across

Opposite: Pvt. Church H. Smith of the 46th Illinois Infantry drew this sketch of the Warren County jail, complete with a shell bursting over it. (Merle and Cathy Messerschmidt)

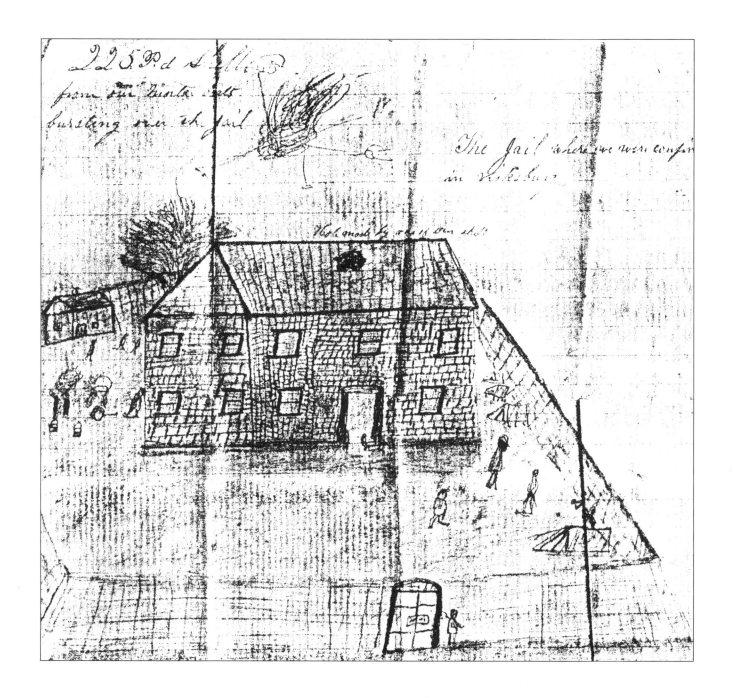

the River at daylight next morning and as he was their agent we knew it must be It had been an eventful day to us for we had heard nearly every cannon they had belch forth their thunders when the Gallant old Cincinati was maintaining the unequal contest and we heard their yells which confirmed what our jailor told us that she was sinking soon after one of his crew they had captured came in where we was and told us of it Well night came after a while and before daylight had made its appearance we were all in Ranks and marching down to the Levee where as soon as light we were convoyed across the River. We were not much sorry to leave Vicksburg but we were much glad to get into our lines again. . . . We gave all of our clothes a good washing for our stay in V'g gave us lice by the wholesale. . . ."

—Pvt. Church H. Smith
Company A, 46th Illinois Infantry,
captured the night of May 25, 1863

This poem appeared in the *Vicksburg Daily Herald,* a Union newspaper published during the occupation, on November 10, 1864. (OCHM)

The Vicksburg Jail.

We have received the following "pome" from a gentleman now sojourning in this hospitable mansion. We are always willing to assist the struggling muse, especially when in difficulties like those which surround this poet; but we have always considered it very bad taste to speak ill of your hotel, and would advise this son of Neptune to make himself comfortable, and live on friendly terms with the rats and other folks who are also tenants of this excellent institution:

THE VICKSBURG JAIL.

WRITTEN AND COMPOSED BY A MARINE.

O, when the poar pris'ner is put in the jaile,
He is put in a cell and his doors are all bar'd;
With a great long chane he is bound to the floor,
And dam thear mean soles thay can do nothing more.

Our beds are maid of old rotten rugs,
And when you lay down you are covered with bugs;
The rugs they will swear they will never give bail,
And you're bound to get lousy in Vicksburg jale.

In the morning you get a piece of bread
As hard as a rock and as heavy as lead,
A cup of cold coffee and meat that is stale,
And you are bound to get hungry in the Vicksburg jale.

Our jury they are a mighty mean crew,
Thay will look at a man as if thay would look him through;
The Judge he will prattle, all hell he don't fear,
He will bring you in guilty if you prove yourself clear.

Our Stats Arturny are men of renown,
Thay spend all theur time in lofing around,
Your pockets they will pick and your cloths will sell,
Get drunk on the mony, that is doing well.

The jailor comes round at nine in the night,
In one of his hands he carrys a light,
He will rap at your door and give you a bale
To see that you're safe in the Vicksburg jale.

Oh, honrably kind friends i have finish'd my song,
i hope i have song to you nothing that is wrong;
For fighting and drinking i never did fail,
And i don't give a dam for the Vicksburg jale.

Some of the first reinforcements to appear were Gen. John Gregg and his brigade of Texas and Tennessee troops, who arrived in Jackson on May 8. On the eleventh, Gregg was ordered by Pemberton to march to Raymond and watch for a small group of Federal raiders who were detached from the main army and headed in his direction. Unknown to Gregg, the Yankees bearing down on his small force of 4,000 men were not a small party of raiders but McPherson's 17th Corps, 12,000 men strong.

At about ten o'clock in the morning, the Federal vanguard was hit by volleys from Gregg's Confederates, who were deployed in line of battle behind Fourteen Mile Creek. Because of the great clouds of dust and smoke, Gregg did not realize the size of the enemy force and launched an attack on the Federals. McPherson was also in the dark as to the size of the Confederate force, thinking it much larger than it actually was. The fighting raged back and forth along Fourteen Mile Creek for hours before the superior Union numbers broke the Confederate line and Gregg had to withdraw his men from the battlefield and march back toward Jackson and safety. The fight had been a very bloody one for its size, with 442 Federal casualties and 514 Confederate casualties. Capt. Patrick M. Griffin of the 10th Tennessee Infantry, in reminiscing about the battle, said of Raymond, "Lord! We learned what war meant that day."

The Battle of Raymond was a small engagement, but it caused some profound changes in Grant's plan. The hard fight put up by Gregg and his men led Grant to believe that there was a large force of Rebels in Jackson. If he stuck to his original plan and tried to cut the Southern Railroad near Edwards, he would be turning his back on a powerful foe in Jackson and inviting an attack on his rear. The solution to a fighter like Grant was obvious: "I therefore determined to move swiftly towards Jackson, destroy

Ketchum Hand Grenade sent home by Capt. William M. Baker (OCHM)

I send a hand grenade which was thrown against our men as they were at work in the rifle pits here. It did not explode. It was filled with powder, & on the forward end where the lead is there was a cap so placed that it must inevitably strike upon it as it fell & explode the powder. The stick behind had paper wings in the clefts so that however it was thrown it would inevitably fall on the right end.

—Capt. William Melville Baker
chaplain, 97th Illinois Infantry
Vicksburg, July 28, 1863,
extract from a letter to his wife

61

or drive any force in that direction, and then turn upon Pemberton."

His mind made up, Grant quickly fired orders to his corps commanders on the night of May 12. McPherson at Raymond was to have his 12,000 men march at first light for Clinton, then turn east on the Clinton-Jackson road and march for the capitol city. Sherman and his 15th Corps, then seven miles west of Raymond, was to march before dawn on the Mississippi Springs road that would take him into Jackson from the southeast. McClernand was to move his 17th Corps from their camps near Edwards to Raymond and be in place to act as a reserve. McPherson and Sherman marched their corps all day on the thirteenth, and by nightfall, Grant had nearly 24,000 men within a few hours' marching time of Jackson.

In Jackson the night of May 13, Gen. Joseph E. Johnston arrived to take personal command of the Rebel forces in the city. Commander of the Department of Tennessee and Mississippi, Johnston was Pemberton's immediate superior and had received orders from Jefferson Davis to go to Mississippi and personally take charge of the effort to defeat Grant.

Soon after his arrival, Johnston met with John Gregg and received the grim news that only 6,000 Confederates were on hand to defend the capitol city of Mississippi. The news only got worse, as Gregg related that a Union corps was marching on Jackson from the east. At this point, only McPherson's corps had been spotted by the Confederates; Sherman's corps coming up from the southeast was still undetected.

On learning this information, Johnston sent a telegram to the secretary of war in Richmond, stating, "I am too late." Johnston seemed to think that disaster was inevitable and wanted to make sure the blame was not fixed on him.

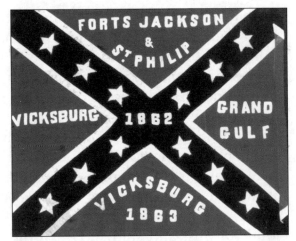

This flag, thought to belong to the First Louisiana Heavy Artillery, has battle honors for Vicksburg in 1862 and 1863. It is in the Old Court House Museum Collections.

Soon after his telegram to Richmond, Johnston came to the conclusion that Jackson had to be abandoned. To give the garrison time to escape, and remove as much war material as possible, Johnston ordered Gregg to take 2,500 men and fight a delaying action to slow the Union advance. On receipt of this order, Gregg deployed 900 men at the O. P. Wright Farm, three miles northwest of Jackson on the Jackson-Clinton road to meet the known threat from McPherson's corps, still unaware of Sherman's men moving on the city.

At ten o'clock A.M. on May 14, McPherson's vanguard made contact with the Rebels at the Wright Farm, and after a delay of about an hour because of a heavy rainstorm, the bluecoats launched their attack. The Federals charged into the Rebel line and the fighting was hand to hand before the outnumbered graybacks were forced to retreat back into the Jackson defenses. The Federals were unable to mount an immediate pursuit, as their attacking units had been disorganized in the fighting.

Meanwhile, Sherman and his corps were near the southeastern outskirts of the city when they were finally spotted by the Rebels. Gregg hastily assembled a small force to slow the new threat and sent them off. The Confederates took up a position behind Lynch Creek and opened fire on the Union vanguard. The Federals quickly responded and the outmatched Confederates were forced to fall back into the city defenses. Sherman pushed his men forward and found the earthworks to be mostly undefended. He quickly moved his men through one of the undefended sections of the earthworks and soon captured or chased away the remaining Rebels.

Back on the Clinton-Jackson road, McPherson finally got his units reorganized and moving on the Jackson defenses. His lead elements soon found the Rebel works deserted, for at two o'clock

Confederate soldiers, usually short of supplies, took U.S. buckles and wore them upside down, saying the initials stood for "Southern Nation." They are from the Old Court House Museum Collections.

P.M., General Gregg was informed that the last Confederate supplies had left the city headed for Canton, and considering his job done, he ordered his men to evacuate the city.

The Battle of Jackson was over, and the United States flag once more flew over the capitol of Mississippi. The Union army had taken the city at very little cost—41 killed and 251 wounded. Gregg's Confederates had taken a total of 845 casualties during their successful delaying action.

Grant now set his sights on the goal that had eluded him for so long: Vicksburg. Orders went out to McClernand and McPherson, telling them to move their men west the next morning to Bolton. Sherman was to remain behind in Jackson with his corps and destroy anything of military value.

On the day that Jackson fell, Pemberton was engaged in trying to mass his army at Edwards. The general had under his command at this point an army of five divisions, approximately 32,000 men. Pemberton's five division commanders were Gens. John Bowen, Martin Luther Smith, Carter L. Stevenson, William W. Loring, and John Forney.

Pemberton had with him at Edwards only 22,000 of his men— he had left Forney's and Smith's divisions behind to protect Vicksburg. Pemberton had been charged by Jefferson Davis to defend Vicksburg at all costs, and the safety of the Hill City was of great concern to the general.

On May 14, Pemberton received orders from Johnston to move his army east to Clinton, and the two Rebel commanders could combine their forces to destroy any enemy in the vicinity. Pemberton, however, was still very worried about the safety of Vicksburg and, after a conference with his division commanders, decided on a different course of action. Pemberton ordered his army to move to the southeast, with the objective of cutting the

Gen. John C. Pemberton, defender of Vicksburg

Grand Gulf-Raymond road that ran between those two towns. This road was the lifeline for Grant's army, and with it cut, Grant would have to come out and fight on ground of Pemberton's choosing.

Pemberton started his movement the morning of May 15, and throughout the day, the long gray column was plagued with delays that made for a very long and fatiguing march. The column wound its way past Champion Hill, one of the most prominent features in the area, and by nightfall, the head of the column was on the Raymond Road when Pemberton called a halt to the march, and the soldiers bedded down for some much-needed rest. George Bradley of Company F, 5th Missouri Infantry (C.S.) later said of this night, "I never can forget the awful stillness that pervaded the rest of that night so many brave and noble men laying in line of battle thinking and dreaming of home and loved ones for the last time."

While the Rebels were making their slow march to the Raymond Road on the fifteenth, McPherson's and McClernand's blue columns were swiftly moving west. By nightfall nearly 32,000 Union soldiers were within striking distance of Pemberton's army.

On the morning of May 16, Pemberton received orders from Johnston again directing him to try and affect a linkup between the two Rebel armies. This time Pemberton decided to comply, but the advancing Union army made this impossible, so there was no choice but to fight. The Union army moved on Pemberton in three parallel columns: McPherson's corps on the Jackson Road to the north and McClernand's corps split with part of his force in the center on the appropriately named Middle Road and the rest on the Raymond Road to the south.

Pemberton deployed his army with Carter Stevenson's division on the left, defending Champion Hill and the Middle Road; Loring's division was on the right, defending the Raymond Road; and

General Grant's headquarters was a tent until after the surrender, when he moved into a Vicksburg mansion. (OCHM)

Bowen's division in the center, protecting the Ratliff Road, which connected the Middle and Raymond roads. The Confederates occupied a strong position, but their inferiority of numbers forced Pemberton to stretch his line very thin to cover the area he had to defend.

At ten thirty A.M. the battle began in earnest as McPherson sent 10,000 of his men forward to attack the Confederate defenders of Champion Hill. In savage fighting, the Confederate position was smashed and the Rebels forced back in great disorder. By one o'clock, the Confederate left flank was in danger of collapse, and Pemberton was forced to call on General Bowen to bring his troops and attack the advancing Federals.

Bowen's men were some of the best combat veterans in either army, and they smashed into the Federals with a fury, driving the Yankees before them. Missourian George Bradley recalled this attack with great sadness in his memoirs, saying, "We charged one charge after another for about two miles running over the dead and wounded of both sides it was a heart rendering sight to see so many brave and noble men who a few hours before well and hearty now dead and dying and wounded in every conceivable way."

Bowen's men pressed on, recapturing the crest of Champion Hill and, for a moment, threatened to break through the Union line. Just when Bowen's men were on the verge of success, Union reinforcements thrown into the fight stopped the Rebels in their tracks and then slowly pushed them off of the ground they had paid so dearly for with men's lives.

Bowen's men were forced to retreat hurriedly because McClernand's corps had finally started moving on the Middle Road, and they were threatening to cut off the Rebels from their retreat route. Confederate James T. Kidd remembered the retreat

Men of the 8th Wisconsin Infantry brought with them to Vicksburg an eagle mascot, Old Abe, and the unit had an eagle bearer as well as flag bearers. Confederates thought the eagle a female and called it "Old Abigail." (OCHM)

as "Horses running, men falling, cannon and small arms roaring. Surely some great guiding hand carried me through."

With Bowen's attack repulsed, Pemberton realized the battle was lost and that he had to get his army safely off the battlefield. This meant he had to get his men across Baker's Creek to his rear before they were cut off and trapped by the Federals. Pemberton ordered Loring to cover the retreat and delay the Union army so that the Confederates could get across the creek to safety.

Loring successfully carried out his delaying mission, but in the process, his division was cut off by the Federals and unable to get across the creek with the rest of the Rebel army. To get away, Loring turned his division south and marched away from the battlefield. His men spent an exhausting three days marching around the Federal army to make it back to Jackson, which had been reoccupied by Johnston after the Yankees left the city.

Champion Hill had been a terrible bloodletting for both sides, as casualty figures reflected: the Confederates had 381 killed and 1,018 wounded, the Federals 410 killed and 1,844 wounded. Chaplain R. L. Howard of the 124th Illinois Infantry probably summed up the feelings of many of his fellow soldiers when he wrote, "We covered ourselves with glory, but at the cost of many precious lives."

The night of May 16, 1863, found Pemberton's army in full retreat following the Battle of Champion Hill. Safety for them was seven miles away at the Big Black River, where the Confederates had entrenchments on the east side of the river. Upon reaching the Big Black, Stevenson's division crossed over and went into camp for the night. When Bowen's division arrived, it was sent into the entrenchments on the east side of the river, along with a brigade of fresh troops who had not fought at Champion Hill. Pemberton had left some of his troops on the east side of the river

The Battle of Champion Hill, some historians believe, is where the war was won—or lost. *(Harper's Weekly)*

because the general was unaware that Loring's divison had not followed the rest of the retreating army. Pemberton believed Loring was bringing up the rear, and he wanted to keep the Big Black crossing open so that Loring would not be trapped on the east side.

The next day, May 17, Grant pushed his eager troops west after the Rebels. Sherman's corps had caught up with Grant after completing the destruction of Jackson, so the Union army was at full strength for the final push on Vicksburg.

McClernand's corps made contact with Bowen's Rebels on the morning of the seventeenth, and the Union general quickly formed his men for an attack on the Confederate entrenchments. The brigade of Gen. Michael K. Lawler charged the Confederate works and smashed through them, creating a fatal rupture in the Rebel line. For the Confederates there was nothing left to do but make an all-out run for the Big Black River crossings. Many of the Rebels were cut off by the Federals and faced with the choice of swimming the Big Black or surrendering to the enemy. Onc soldier who had to make the choice, James T. Kidd, said of the situation, "At any rate, the bridge was set on fire and about 2200 of our troops were cut off. I with the rest could do nothing but surrender, - Black River in front, Grant's army in the rear. Between hell and the deep sea."

The Union army won a sweeping victory at the Big Black River: with total casualties of less than 300, they had taken 1,800 Confederate prisoners and captured 18 cannon. But more important to Grant was the fact that the goal he had fought so hard to attain was near at hand; the next stop for his blue-clad soldiers was fortress Vicksburg.

After their defeat at the Big Black River, Pemberton's men had only one thought on their minds—to get back to Vicksburg as fast

Concrete piers marked the site of the railroad bridge across the Big Black River near Bovina after the Battle of Big Black. (OCHM)

[See page 70.]

WIFE'S MOURNING WAS PREMATURE

Maj. G. W. Fly could hardly believe it: a courier had just arrived at Camp Timmons, a few miles north of Vicksburg, with news that the major's wife and children were in town, registered at a hotel and hoping to see him.

Only a week earlier, Mrs. Fly had been in mourning, for Texas newspapers had reported her husband killed at Corinth. She never received the letters he had written, so she had no reason to doubt the story of his death—until a local soldier arrived at home in Gonzales County, Texas, after being discharged in Vicksburg. When the young man met Mrs. Fly on the street, he was curious as to why she was dressed in black. After hearing her story he assured her that he had seen the major the previous week, and he was very much alive and in good health.

Almost afraid to believe the good news, Mrs. Fly decided to put her mind at ease, to travel to Vicksburg to see if her husband was really alive. Despite the protestations of her family and friends, she undertook the hazardous trip across Texas and Louisiana in a two-horse wagon, crossing the river at Rodney, some forty-five miles south of Vicksburg, then making her way upriver for the reunion with Major Fly.

Happily reunited, Major Fly arranged for his wife and children to board with a local family not far from his camp.

Though Mrs. Fly drove a wagon all the way to Vicksburg from Texas, railroad tracks extended west of Vicksburg to Monroe, Louisiana. Originally the Alabama and Vicksburg, the company expanded, and the name changed by 1860 to the Southern Railroad Company, which printed its own script. (OCHM)

Before firing this Minié ball at the Confederates near the railroad redoubt, the Union soldier carved a message on it: "FROM GRANT." It is part of the Old Court House Museum Collections.

as possible. It was every man for himself, and the Rebel army dissolved into a mass of individuals running for the Vicksburg defenses.

The beaten men of Pemberton's army began to stream into Vicksburg on the afternoon of the seventeenth, and the sight was never forgotten by the civilians who witnessed the sight. Dora Richards Miller said of the sad procession, "About three o'clock the rush began. I shall never forget that woeful sight of a beaten, demoralized army that came rushing back, - humanity in the last throes of endurance. Wan, hollow-eyed, ragged, footsore, bloody, the men limped along unarmed, but followed by siege guns, ambulances, gun carriages, and wagons in aimless confusion. At twilight two or three bands on the court house hill and other points began playing Dixie, Bonnie Blue Flag, and so on, and drums began to beat all about; I suppose they were rallying the scattered army."

With the men safe in the Vicksburg defenses, work quickly began to reorganize the army and get ready for the blue-clad host that was bearing down on them. The strength of the Vicksburg defenses they now occupied did wonders for the morale of the Rebel soldiers. They may have been defeated thus far in the campaign, but they still had some fight left in them and were ready to have another go at the Yankees.

The city of Vicksburg was completely encircled on the landward side by earthwork entrenchments running some eight miles, from Fort Hill in the north to South Fort below the city. The defenses of the city were further strengthened by a series of nine earthwork forts along the line, protecting the areas of advance an enemy would use to try and enter the city.

In these formidable works Pemberton had 30,000 soldiers and 172 pieces of artillery to defend the city of Vicksburg. Of his

30,000 men, two divisions—Smith's and Forney's—were fresh, having remained behind to protect the city when Pemberton went out to confront Grant.

Pemberton deployed his men in the Vicksburg entrenchments with Smith's division to the north, Forney's division in the center, and Stevenson's division to the south. Bowen's division, those fierce Westerners that had so nearly won the day at Champion Hill, were held in reserve to be used wherever needed.

At sunset on May 18, 1863, the vanguard of the Union army reached the outskirts of Vicksburg. Grant began moving his men into position to attack, with Sherman's corps to the north, McPherson's corps in the center, and McClernand's corps to the south. Despite the strength of the Rebel defenses, Grant believed the Confederates were demoralized from their recent defeats and could not withstand a direct assault.

As a result of Grant's belief that the Confederates would not put up much of a fight, at two o'clock P.M. on May 19, he ordered an attack, even though most of his troops were not in place to make the assault. The offensive was carried out for the most part by Sherman's corps, and the focal point of their attack was the Stockade Redan, an earthwork fort protecting the Graveyard Road entrance into Vicksburg.

As Sherman's men advanced on the redan, their ranks were staggered by the destructive volleys poured into them by the Rebel defenders. The Yankees pressed the attack with great valor, and some even reached the Confederate works. But at no point were the defenses breached, and at the end of the day, all Grant had to show for his efforts was a large casualty list—157 killed, 777 wounded.

After the killing had ended for the day, Capt. William Larkin Faulk of Company B, 38th Mississippi Infantry recorded in his

Soldiers from North and South met to bury the dead several days after Grant's unsuccessful assault on May 22, 1863. (*Battles and Leaders*)

diary, "We have fought the enemy very hard today and held our positions well along the line. I thank almighty God for his protection through the past days."

Although his first attempt to take Vicksburg had been repulsed, Grant still believed his troops could take the city by storm. He prepared his men for a larger and more coordinated attack that would make full use of his powerful army.

At ten o'clock A.M. on May 22, the order to attack was given, and all three Union corps began to move on the Confederate works. The focus of the Union attack was the forts defending the entrances to the city, and they were the scenes of some of the bloodiest fighting of the campaign. Forts with names like Stockade Redan, 3rd Louisiana Redan, Great Redoubt, 2nd Texas Lunette, and Railroad Redoubt were written into the history books in the blood of the men who fought and died for them.

At the Stockade Redan, the first Union troops to advance were 150 men carrying planks and scaling ladders, with the mission to bridge the ditch in front of the fort and throw ladders on the walls so the next wave of infantry could scale the parapet. Dubbed the "forlorn hope" because of their slim chance of survival, volunteers were called for to undertake this hazardous duty, and only unmarried men were accepted from the throngs of men that freely offered to risk their lives.

The Rebels poured a terrible fire into the forlorn hope, inflicting very heavy casualties. A few survivors reached the ditch in front of the redan and were pinned there until nightfall by the heavy fire.

At 2:15 P.M. a second Union assault wave was sent into the fight at the Stockade Redan. The Yankees were again met with withering volleys from the Rebels, and they left a trail of blue-clad bodies to mark their path of advance. The bravery displayed by the Federals

The Marine hospital was constructed before the war by the Federal government to treat those who became ill while employed on the river. It was operated by the Confederates during the siege. (*Harper's Weekly*)

This Confederate battery was located near the Marine hospital on the waterfront. (OCHM)

[See page 74.]

"SHE STILL HELD THE TINY AND BLOODY HAND . . ."

During a lull in the bombardment, a young mother emerged with her small daughter from one of the caves. The child, romping in the fresh air and sunshine, rushed to a nearby field where some flowers were blooming.

Eagerly, the child plucked a tender blossom with a tiny hand.

At that instant, the Yankee shelling was resumed and the horror-stricken young mother grasped her child's hand and started running for the shelter of the cave.

A falling shell exploded near them, tearing a crater in the soft earth.

The mother looked down. In her own hand she still held the tiny and bloody hand of her child, which had been torn from the baby's body.

The white blossom was still clutched between the tiny fingers, but now its color was crimson.

—Deana J. Olcott
*Historical Jottings of
Port Gibson, Mississippi*

This recently discovered photograph is marked on the reverse with the name "Ward" and also "Victim of Vicksburg bombardment." The 1860 census of Vicksburg lists a Ward couple, T. F. and Anna C., who were twenty-two and eighteen, respectively; he was from Pennsylvania, she from Ireland. Note the child's right arm is missing. Could she be the one described above? (Giambrone Collection)

After Union soldiers stole a silver service from Ellen Batchelor at Hoboken Plantation east of Vicksburg, Gen. Peter Osterhaus found it and had it returned to her. When the Batchelor home burned in later years, this piece, from the Old Court House Museum Collections, was all that was saved. (Pickett Photography)

in the attack made quite an impression on the Rebels, and years later Capt. James H. Jones of Company D, 38th Mississippi Infantry wrote with admiration about the courage displayed by the Union soldiers: "As they came down the hill one could see them plunging headlong to the front, and as they rushed up the slope to our works they invariably fell backwards, as the death shot greeted them. They came into the very jaws of death and died. Surely no more desperate courage than this could be displayed by mortal men."

At other points along the line, McPherson's and McClernand's men fought with similar valor but suffered equally high casualties with little to show for their losses. McClernand's men did manage to take some of the outer Confederate works, but they were unable to make a decisive breakthrough.

Nightfall brought an end to the fighting on May 22, and again all Grant had to show for his efforts was more Federal casualties: 502 men were killed and 2,550 were wounded against Confederate casualties of less than 500.

With his second attack on the Vicksburg defenses ending in a bloody repulse, Grant acknowledged the city could not be taken by direct assault. He decided to besiege the city and starve the Confederates into submission. Union soldiers put down their muskets and took up spades and shovels and began digging entrenchments that would eventually encircle the Confederate fortifications in a viselike grip from which none could escape.

Into these earthworks Grant placed 220 cannon that threw shot and shell at the Confederate entrenchments night and day to wear down the defenders. Sharpshooters did a deadly business on both sides of the line as they hunted for men careless enough to expose themselves over the works. The war now became a waiting game in the trenches for the rank and file of both armies, with the threat of death a constant companion.

Capt. James H. Jones vividly described the grim reality of siege life when he wrote, "Day by day, as the siege progressed, it was the sole business of the soldier to kill or be killed. Day by day some friend or comrade died, and 'who next?' was on every man's lips and in every man's heart, only to be answered by the thud of a bullet or the crash of a shell."

As the war at the front lines went on, there was a second war going on for the civilians trapped within the besieged city. For all intents and purposes, the people of Vicksburg, men, women, and children, were on the front lines as they were exposed to the hail of shot and shell being thrown into the city, just like any Confederate soldier in the entrenchments. These civilians were literally caught between two fires—Union shells overshot the Confederate line, screaming into the city, and from the Mississippi River the U.S. Navy sent a constant stream of shells into Vicksburg.

To protect themselves from the storm of iron being thrown at them, the people had to dig caves into the soft loam of the Vicksburg hills. Most of these caves were simple affairs, just large enough to shelter a single family, but they were very effective—less than twenty civilians died in Vicksburg during the siege.

Despite the constant threat from the shelling, life did go on in Vicksburg. Christ Episcopal Church was open for services every day, and St. Paul Catholic Church held services sporadically during the siege. Editor James Swords continued to publish his newspaper, the *Daily Citizen,* even though he had run out of newsprint. The ingenious editor published at least seven issues, printing his news on the back of unused wallpaper.

On hearing of a young woman killed by a shell, Swords vented his anger on the Federals in the June 25 issue of the *Citizen,* saying that "We have learned of but one casualty resulting from the

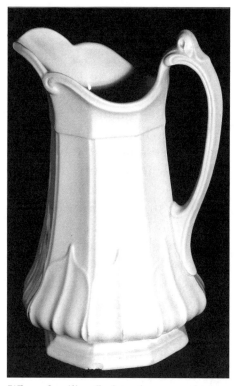

When families fled to the caves during the siege, they often took household items with them. Mr. and Mrs. Alex Legrand used this water pitcher, which is in the Old Court House Museum Collections.

[See page 79.]

75

BLAST LITERALLY BLEW ABRAHAM TO FREEDOM

Once the dust and dirt settled, the clods stopped falling and the smoke cleared, Abraham was found lying on a pile of dirt "in a most disturbed state of mind."

How far had the blast blown him? "Don't know, master, but think 'bout three mile," he told the men gathered round him.

The incident occurred on June 25, 1863, when powder was exploded in a tunnel Union soldiers had dug beneath the 3rd Louisiana Redan, not far from the Shirley House, now in the Vicksburg National Military Park.

The result was that the top of the hill was blown off and a crater created, but the opening wasn't large enough for Yankee troops to rush through to create a breach in the Rebel lines.

Though the Confederates had been busy digging their own tunnel to try and find the Yankee sappers, they had also thrown up a line of works behind the 3rd Louisiana Redan, and because of their foresight, only about half a dozen were killed or injured.

Though Gen. U. S. Grant wrote that Abraham wasn't much hurt but "terribly frightened," Dr. Silas T. Trowbridge, chief surgeon of the 3rd Division, 17th Army Corps, recalled that the man was "badly bruised, and for some days I thought his chances to live very doubtful. He fell on soft ground, and evidently on the back part of his head and shoulders, as there were the most serious injuries."

Soon, Dr. Trowbridge said, Gen. John A. Logan wanted to see Abraham.

After some routine questions, Logan asked Abraham, "What did you mean by fighting us who are the friends of the black man?"

"I wasn't fit'n you, sir," he replied.

"But did you not have a gun and shoot at the Yanks?" Logan persisted.

"No sir. 'Fore God, no sir," Abraham defended himself.

Abraham was badly bruised but alive following the explosion at the crater. (*Harper's Weekly*)

Union soldiers worked on one side of the hill and Confederates on the other, each digging a tunnel, the Yankees planning to blow up the earthworks with a mine and the Rebels trying to stop them. *(Harper's Weekly)*

Logan wanted to know where Abraham had been at the time of the explosion, and he told the general he had been sleeping in the shade near the breastworks. Why had he not held onto something? Logan asked, and Abraham told Logan what he had said to others—that he was blown into the air about three miles.

Present as the detonating of the explosives in the tunnel was Theodore R. Davis, an artist with *Harper's Weekly Magazine,* who drew a picture of Abraham. Davis said Abraham was blown about 300 yards and told the artist that he asked a white man "whare wese going, and the next thing I knowed he was nowhere but all over."

After Davis completed his sketch, Abraham scrutinized it for a moment, broke into a laugh, and proclaimed the likeness "this child for shore." Then he asked for a quarter.

"One of General McPherson's staff, Col. Coolbaugh, bestowed a silver half" upon the man who ran as fast as he could "in a style showing that he was but little the worse for his aerial voyage," Davis wrote.

Abraham hung around the Union camp, working as a servant for Dr. Trowbridge for about a month, but the good physician was not pleased with Abraham's service, as the man never "comprehended the regularity of any of my wants."

"To have invented such unsophisticated stupidity as he constantly exercised much transcended the capacity of any human being," Trowbridge wrote in his memoirs in 1872. "Poor Abe was the dumbest mortal I ever saw."

The last time Abraham appears in the records was when he was in Atlanta, working as a cook on the staff of Gen. James B. McPherson. After the general's death, Abraham vanished from recorded history. He had made his mark in Vicksburg, however, when he was literally blown from slavery to freedom.

After Union troops detonated the powder, they poured into the breach that the explosion created, but the Confederates, in a fierce counterattack, held them back and kept them from penetrating any further. (Headley's *Great Rebellion*, II)

shelling—Miss Holly who was killed in the suburbs of the city. Further than this they can have little to boast, although hozannahs of the damned would be uttered from their black throats could they murder the whole of the women and children now within our defenses."

Back on the front lines, the grim business of siege warfare continued. On June 25, Grant tried a new tactic, exploding a mine under the 3rd Louisiana Redan and then sending an assault force into the breach caused by the explosion. The fighting raged for just over a day, but the Yankees were unable to achieve a breakthrough and withdrew their forces from the crater.

As the siege wore on, one of the main concerns of the Rebels was getting enough food to eat. The rations being issued were continually being reduced, and the men were always hungry. Memories of the lack of food compelled Robert L. Bachman of Company G, 60th Tennessee Infantry to write in his memoir "Remembrance of my hungry days in the trenches at Vicksburg will always move me to feed any hungry man who comes my way, however much of a tramp he may be."

As June gave way to July, and with his men growing steadily weaker each day from lack of food, Pemberton was forced to seek terms of surrender from Grant on July 3. Under the terms of surrender, officers were allowed to keep their side arms and the horses they owned. The most significant term, however, was that all the Confederate soldiers were paroled and not sent to Northern prison camps.

At ten o'clock A.M. on July 4, 1863, the Rebel defenders of Vicksburg marched out in front of the earthworks they had defended faithfully to the bitter end, stacked their arms, and furled their torn and tattered flags for the last time. Having to surrender was bad enough, but doing it on the Fourth of July was a

Pvt. F. M. Lassiter of Company I, 28th Mississippi Cavalry, was a teenage soldier when he was paroled from Vicksburg. (OCHM)

bitter blow to the Confederates. Captain Faulk sadly recorded in his diary "How humiliating it is for us to be compelled to submit to such an enemy, and that too on the 4th of July; but we have done all that men could do — we held them 48 [47] days on very scant rations and we would have continued to hold the place had our rations held out."

Once the surrender was completed, victorious Union troops marched into Vicksburg to take possession of the city. They raised the Stars and Stripes over the Warren County Court House, and this symbol of Federal might could be seen for miles around by the citizens of Vicksburg.

The campaign for the city of Vicksburg exacted a terrible toll from the soldiers on both sides of the conflict. Federal losses amounted to 1,581 killed, 7,554 wounded, and 1,007 missing. Confederate casualties were nearly as high: 1,413 killed, 3,878 wounded, and 3,800 missing.

On July 11, with their paroles completed, the Confederates marched out of Vicksburg and slowly made their way back to their homes and families. For a short precious time, the men were on furlough and free from the war. But all too soon, duty would call them back to battle in defense of the South. The Rebels had been beaten at Vicksburg, but they were not yet defeated. The same fighting spirit that had sustained them through forty-seven days of siege would sustain them through two more years of bloody warfare.

A marble shaft intended to mark the grave of a Mexican War veteran was taken from a local tombstone company, carved with appropriate information, and placed at the surrender site in 1864. Chipped by souvenir hunters, it was later removed and an upright cannon barrel used in its place. The shaft is now in the Visitor's Center of the Vicksburg National Military Park. (OCHM)

Opposite page: In a romanticized painting by Howard Johnson of Corinth, Mississippi, General Pemberton tells his weary soldiers that he is on his way to talk to General Grant about terms of surrender. The painting is in the Old Court House Museum Collections. (Pickett Photography)

Union troops paraded around the courthouse on July 4, 1863, and were reviewed by General Grant. Contrary to the liberties taken by the Northern artist, no one turned out to welcome them. The drawing shows some damage near the roofline in the corner. Not until 1869 was the hill terraced and a brick-retaining wall constructed around court square. *(Frank Leslie's Illustrated)*

"NO SAFETY ANYWHERE," MRS. BALFOUR WROTE

I have stayed at home every night except two. I could not stand the mosquitoes and the crowd in the caves. Most people spend their time entirely in them, for there is no safety anywhere else. Indeed, there is no safety there. Several were killed or crippled. . . .

* * * *

I walked there [to Christ Episcopal Church] and back—but I was glad to do so for the sake of worshipping once more. The church has been considerably injured and was so filled with bricks, mortar and glass that it was difficult to find a place to sit.

* * * *

Last night was one long to be remembered in the annals of our little city. In addition to the usual shelling from the bombs and Parrott guns, there was a terrible fire in town. Nearly the whole of the block from Brown and Johnston to Cruther's Store burned, only two houses left. . . . It was an awful and strange sight. As I sat at my window, I saw the mortars from the west passing entirely over the house and the Parrott shells from the east passing by, crossing each other, and this terrible fire raging in the center.

* * * *

The general impression is that they fire at the city. . . . thinking that they will wear out the women and children and sick, and General Pemberton will be obliged to surrender the place on that account; but they little know the spirit of the Vicksburg women and children if they expect this. Rather than let them know they are causing us any suffering I would be content to suffer martyrdom!

—Emma Balfour's diary
May 27, 30-31, June 2, 1863

Emma Harrison Balfour, famed diarist

"WHISTLING DICK" MOST FAMOUS REBEL CANNON

The battlefield at Vicksburg was rocked by the crash and thunder of hundreds of artillery pieces during the forty-seven-day siege, but for the Union soldiers, one sound stood out among all the others: a whistling messenger of death in the form of a Rebel shell that dealt terrible destruction in the Federal ranks.

The cannon that fired these shells was the Confederate gun known as "Whistling Dick," probably the most famous of the Vicksburg siege guns. It was a rifled eighteen-pounder cannon that fired a projectile described by Rebel artilleryman A. L. Slack as "a connical, parrott-like shell which made a whirring noise when fired and was dubbed 'Whistling Dick' by the suggestive soldier who gave it this phonetic name."

The famed gun was served by the men of Company E, 1st Louisiana Heavy Artillery in the defenses overlooking the Mississippi River. It was used in this position from May 18 to the twenty-second, when it was temporarily put out of action in a duel with Union gunboats.

The Louisianans manning the gun were ordered to move it on May 28 to an earthwork in rear of Gen. Stephen D. Lee's brigade. The gun served faithfully in this position until the end of the siege.

Whistling Dick was so well known during the siege that Federals all along the lines thought the famous gun was being fired at them. One of the guns that the Yankees had mistaken for Dick was another famously named gun, the "Widow Blakely," so named because the 7.44-inch Blakely Rifle was the only one of its type in the Vicksburg defenses.

connical, parrott-like shell . . . made a whirring noise when fired . . .

84

CONFEDERATES SILENTLY CONSIGNED WHISTLING DICK TO A WATERY GRAVE

Lt. Simeon Martin of the 46th Mississippi Infantry wrote in his memoirs that he talked with a Federal artillery captain after the surrender who testified to the accuracy of Whistling Dick, of the destruction and death that resulted from it, and the terror in which the gun was held. Practically every Northern soldier wanted to see the famous gun.

No Federal was destined to see Whistling Dick—the cannoneers had a strong affection for the cannon, and, Martin wrote, "When it became apparent that all our efforts were to be fruitless, and that the starved and debilitated but still dauntless garrison of Vicksburg would be compelled to lay down their arms, these gunners swore in their wrath that Dick should never be included in the surrender. It is said that the gunners were true to their word, and that on the night of July 3d, 1863, preceding the surrender on the following day, Dick was consigned to a wattery grave, beneath the waves of the Mighty Father of Waters."

In 1900, the Reverend Alfred P. Leach of Columbus, Mississippi, was in Vicksburg, and he verified what Lieutenant Martin and others thought. Leach had been a member of Company K, 35th Mississippi Infantry during the siege. He had been a sergeant and was detailed along with thirteen other men to dispose of the gun.

"It was on the third of July, 1863, and somewhere between 10 and 11 p.m.," Leach told the *Vicksburg Evening Post*. "I remember it was very dark. We marched into the courthouse and there took an oath not to divulge the secret to the Yankees. It was not until we reached the courthouse that all knew the purpose for which the detail had been gotten together. We marched silently to the river and there at the foot of the street—either Grove or Jackson—found two small coal barges. They were lashed together, end to end, and decked over."

Leach said the men silently sneaked the gun safely aboard, shoved out into the stream until "getting out some distance, we silently dumped the old gun over the end of the barge into the still waters."

Lieutenant Martin recalled that he had heard the story at different times after the surrender; some of the Confederates had talked with the gun crew and heard them say, "If any of the damd Yankees wanted to find Whistling Dick, they would have to look in the bottom of the Mississippi River."

Martin said the barge had shoved out from the foot of Jackson Street, "where he now silently reposes in oblivion, unconscious of the changes above him, and where he will doubtless repose for centuries to come, perchance eventually to be again brought to the surface, by a convulsion of nature or otherwise, and treasured by future generations as a mute relic of the forgotten past."

This captured Confederate gun at the Castle Battery was incorrectly identified as Whistling Dick years after the war. (OCHM)

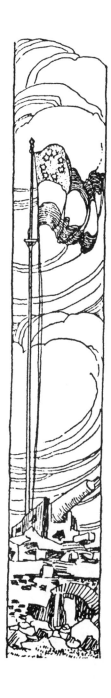

"LET THIS BE A FLAG OF TRUCE"

At first the guard refused to let the lady and her escort see General Grant, but when she burst into tears, he relented, and soon she was seated in the general's headquarters.

She was Mrs. Thomas P. Dockery, wife of an Arkansas Confederate general and was concerned about his safety. Grant heard the lady's story and sent an orderly to find General Dockery. After dinner, with Mrs. Dockery as his guest, Grant wrote a pass for the couple so they could go home to Columbia County, Arkansas.

On the day of their departure, General Grant was watching the entourage of men and officers on their way out of Vicksburg. At his feet was a little white Spitz dog that had attached itself to headquarters, becoming a favorite of the men.

As the Dockerys' carriage drew near, Grant picked up the little dog and handed it to Mrs. Dockery, saying, "Let this be a flag of truce between us, Madam, and may my men possess the courage you have shown during the siege." The dog was from then on called Truce and became greatly loved by the men in gray as it had been by those in blue.

When General Dockery resumed his duties in the Confederate army, he took Truce with him. The dog's keen perception of danger was credited with saving lives, and he became a mascot for the men. When he died, Confederate veterans who had served under the general were pallbearers, placing the silky, snowy, little form in a white satin-lined casket and burying him in the Dockery family graveyard at Lamarine, Arkansas. A stone bearing the simple inscription "Truce" marks the grave.

—Mrs. Nettie Kilgore
in *The History of Columbia County*

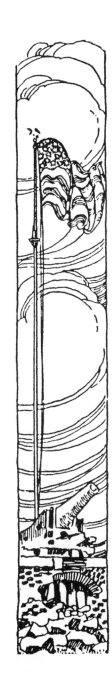

WALLPAPER NEWSPAPER "VALUABLE HEREAFTER"

The masthead proclaimed it to be the *Daily Citizen,* but during the siege of Vicksburg, the newspaper was published sporadically, usually several times a week, for the shortages in the city weren't confined to food and ammunition—there was no newsprint to be had at any price.

James M. Swords, the enterprising editor, was undaunted in the face of adversity, publishing his tabloid pages on wallpaper procured from the stock of a local store. He cut the rolls into foolscap-sized sheets, which he printed on an old hand-fed Franklin Press.

Swords filled the four columns with bits of local news and gossip and accounts from other newspapers that had been smuggled into town. As the war-weary weeks wore on, with no sign of relief, Swords, though a native of Ohio, remained a defiant Rebel. In the last issue— July 2, 1863—he poked fun at General Grant, inserting the following notice:

> *ON DIT—that the great Ulysses—the Yankee Generalissimo, surnamed Grant—has expressed his intentions of dining in Vicksburg on Sunday next, and celebrating the 4th of July by a grand dinner and so forth. When asked if he would invite Gen. Jo. Johnston to join the table he said, 'No! for fear there will be a row at the table! Ulysses must get into the city before he dines in it. The way to cook a rabbit is 'first catch the rabbit, ' etc.*

He put the paper to bed and left the type standing in the chase in his Washington Street shop, where it remained until two days later when victorious Union soldiers swarmed throughout the city. In the newspaper office they found the type just as Swords had left it.

THE DAILY CITIZEN.

J. M. SWORDS, ...Proprietor

VICKSBURG. MISS.

THURSDAY, JULY 2, 1863.

Mrs. Cisco was instantly killed on Monday, on Jackson road. Mrs. Cisco's husband is now in Virginia, a member of Moody's artillery, and the death of such a loving, affectionate and dutiful wife will be a loss to him irreparable.

Opposite page: Editor James M. Swords and his wife, Marie Antoinette Swords, though born in the North, were ardent Confederates. The background for pages 88 and 89 is a copy of an original wallpaper newspaper. (OCHM

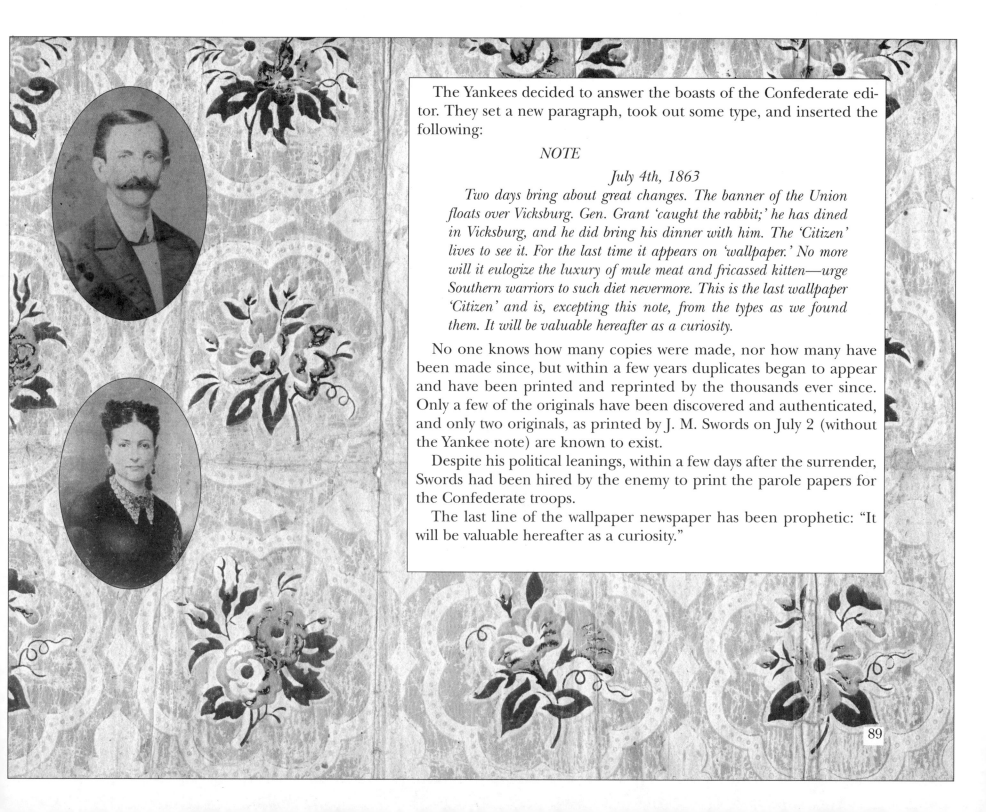

The Yankees decided to answer the boasts of the Confederate editor. They set a new paragraph, took out some type, and inserted the following:

NOTE

July 4th, 1863

Two days bring about great changes. The banner of the Union floats over Vicksburg. Gen. Grant 'caught the rabbit;' he has dined in Vicksburg, and he did bring his dinner with him. The 'Citizen' lives to see it. For the last time it appears on 'wallpaper.' No more will it eulogize the luxury of mule meat and fricassed kitten—urge Southern warriors to such diet nevermore. This is the last wallpaper 'Citizen' and is, excepting this note, from the types as we found them. It will be valuable hereafter as a curiosity.

No one knows how many copies were made, nor how many have been made since, but within a few years duplicates began to appear and have been printed and reprinted by the thousands ever since. Only a few of the originals have been discovered and authenticated, and only two originals, as printed by J. M. Swords on July 2 (without the Yankee note) are known to exist.

Despite his political leanings, within a few days after the surrender, Swords had been hired by the enemy to print the parole papers for the Confederate troops.

The last line of the wallpaper newspaper has been prophetic: "It will be valuable hereafter as a curiosity."

89

CAVES PROVIDED SANCTUARY DURING SIEGE

They weren't natural caves, those caverns in the hillsides where citizens fled for shelter during the bombardment and siege of Vicksburg. Some were hastily dug; others were the pick-and-shovel creations of enterprising entrepreneurs who dug for a fee.

Any place that looked safe from the shelling was a likely spot for a cave, and the underground sanctuaries soon catacombed the hills of the town. Some were little more than holes in the wall; others were of several rooms with front and back entrances. There were caves with bare necessities and others with the luxuries of home.

Sometimes exploding shells loosened the earth, sending showers of dirt raining down on the occupants. Sometimes a deadly messenger of death plunged deep into the ground, collapsing roofs and walls.

Yet, in many respects, life continued much as it had in happier times. There was laughter and heartache, joy and fear; children played; people died. There were at least two births in the caves (one child was appropriately named Siege). In most cases people became accustomed to the routine of cave life, though Emma Balfour, after one night underground, elected to take her chances at home.

Only one cave exists today. Many were filled in during the occupation by orders of General Grant, as he considered them health hazards (and it kept his idle men busy). Others fell victim to time and the bulldozer.

The remaining cave, owned by the Hough family, is almost inaccessible and is on private property. It has two small rooms with a floor plan like a wishbone. Where people once sought safety from withering Yankee fire is now a haven for spiders and possibly an occasional snake. Carved into the wall is a dirt bench where someone probably spent fearful hours praying that the next shell would not make a tomb of his or her shelter.

There were few civilian casualties during the siege—less than a dozen have been verified. Though almost every building in town was damaged, the Civil War bomb shelters had provided safety for most who had fled to them.

Opposite page: Fear grips those living in the caves during the siege when a shell lands nearby, as shown in this illustration from R. G. Horton's *Youth's History.* (Giambrone Collection)

Below: A well-dressed woman kneels in prayer in a cave furnished with some of the luxuries of home as well as the necessities. On the dirt wall in this 1863 drawing is a crucifix. (A. John Volck)

Two monstrous shells fell in a field near the cave where the Lord family lived, shaking the earth and creating a giant crater and filling the air with flames, smoke, and dust. Margaret Lord sought to calm her frightened child, a girl of about four:

"Don't cry, my darling. God will protect us."
"But, mamma," she sobbed, *"I's so 'fraid God's killed too!"*

—W. W. Lord, Jr.
"A Child at the Siege of Vicksburg"
Harper's Monthly Magazine, 1908

"THE CAVE FILLED INSTANTLY WITH POWDER SMOKE AND DUST"

"I was sitting near the entrance, about five o'clock. . . . when the bombardment commenced more furiously than usual, the shells falling thickly around us, causing vast columns of earth to fly upward, mingled with smoke. . . . I was startled by the shouts of the servants and a most fearful jar and rocking of the earth, followed by a deafening explosion, such as I had never heard before. The cave filled instantly with powder smoke and dust. I stood with a tingling, prickling sensation in my head, hands, and feet, and with a confused brain. Yet alive!—was the first glad thought that came to me; - child, servants, all here, and saved!—from some great danger, I felt. I stepped out, to find a group of persons before my cave, looking anxiously for me; and lying all around, freshly torn, rose bushes, arbor-vitae trees, large clods of earth, splinters, pieces of plank, wood, etc. A mortar shell had struck the corner of the cave, fortunately so near the brow of the hill, that it had gone obliquely into the earth, exploding as it went, breaking large masses from the side of the hill—tearing away the fence, the shrubbery and flowers—sweeping all, like an avalanche, down near the entrance of my good refuge. . . .

"That evening some friends sat with me: one took up my guitar and played some pretty little airs for us. . . . How could we sing and laugh amid our suffering fellow beings—amid the shriek of death itself? . . . A little negro child, playing in the yard, had found a shell; in rolling and turning it, had innocently pounded the fuse; the terrible explosion followed, showing, as the white cloud of smoke floated away, the mangled remains of a life that to the mother's heart had possessed all of beauty and joy.

"A young girl, becoming weary in the confinement of the cave, hastily ran to the house in the interval that elapsed between the slowly falling shells. On returning, an explosion sounded near her—one wild scream, and she ran into her mother's presence, sinking like a wounded dove, the life blood flowing over the light summer dress in crimson ripples from a death-wound in her side, caused by the shell fragment.

Mary Loughborough's journal was published in 1864 as *My Cave Life in Vicksburg*. The Missouri diarist had come to the city to be near her husband, a Confederate officer. (OCHM)

92

"A fragment had also struck and broken the arm of a little boy playing near the mouth of his mother's cave. This was one day's account.

"I told of my little girl's great distress when the shells fell thickly near us—how she ran to me breathless, hiding her head in my dress without a word; then cautiously looking out, with her anxious face questioning, would say: 'Oh! mamma, was it a mortar shell?' Poor children, that their little hearts should suffer and quail amidst these daily horrors of war!"

—Mary Loughborough
in *My Cave Life in Vicksburg*

The title page to Mary Loughborough's book depicts the entrance to the cave where she lived. (OCHM)

James M. Loughborough (OCHM)

HERE BROTHERS FOUGHT . . .

In the afternoon [of the Fourth of July 1863] the division to which I belonged marched in and took formal possession. In our regiment was a boy who had a brother in the Rebel Army in Vicksburg. As we came to their works, the brother was there to meet the boy in our regiment. Our boy fell out of ranks, and they walked together, arms around each other's waists. It was a sight most impressive and one to remain vivid a life time—the one in blue with uniform fresh, buttons shining, gun and bayonet bright; the other in gray, ragged uniform, barefoot and grimy. It was enough to make one feel sad that such things had to be.

—Capt. Joel W. Strong
Company I, 10th Missouri
Infantry, U.S.A.

FIREWORKS WERE UNEQUALED

While we were in this camp, the boys having nothing to do, got into the Ordnance Stores of our Army and had a great time with the powder. They would lay trains a hundred yards in length, with a big pile of powder every thirty feet or so, over which they would place a barrel or box. They would then fire the train and when the piles were reached, PLUFF and up would go the box or barrel into the air. They also made a kind of crude Roman Candles, by filling canes with powder, in alternate layers of wet and dry. There were thousands of these, and at night they were flying in every direction; I never saw a civic display of fire-works to equal it.

—Lt. Simeon R. Martin
Company I, 46th Mississippi Infantry
in *Recollections of the War Between the States 1861-1865*

Above: The U.S.S. *Choctaw* led the attack on Haynes Bluff in 1863. This photo, taken probably in late 1863 or early 1864, shows Vicksburg in the background. The hill to the left is where the home the Castle stood; below are the railroad shops, and the first large house to the right, on the hill, is probably the Thomas A. Marshall home. The one next to it is unidentified. *(Review of Reviews)*

Right: The ironclad *Cincinnati* was sunk by Confederate guns at Vicksburg on May 22, 1863, but was salvaged and put back into service. (OCHM)

Right: Dr. Bixby, a Union army physician, took this picture from DeSoto Point, Louisiana, opposite Vicksburg. *(Review of Reviews)*

Below: An unidentified battery. (OCHM)

Moore Vicksburg Miss.

96

This Brooke rifle, made in the Confederacy, was one of two used at Vicksburg in the river batteries and may be the one that helped to sink the *Cincinnati*. (OCHM)

OBSCURE BATTLE WAS CONFEDERATE VICTORY

You won't find Hill's Plantation in the list of Union victories during the Vicksburg Campaign—the fight on June 22, 1863, was won by the Confederates, the only blemish on an otherwise spotless combat record for the Yankees. The small engagement, which in reality was little more than a skirmish, had an effect on Union plans all out of proportion to the size of the fight.

The battle was fought on the high ground just west of the Big Black River, not far from Birdsong's Ferry. Mrs. Fannie Hill, the young widow who owned the plantation, was not at home when the Rebels formed up just across the road from her house to attack a detachment of the 4th Iowa Cavalry.

The seeds of the fight at Hill's Plantation grew out of Grant's concern for the possibility of an attack on the rear of his army. After the Federals had pulled out of Jackson, the city was reoccupied by the Confederates under Gen. Joseph E. Johnston. By June reinforcements to Johnston's army had swelled his numbers to over 30,000 men, enough to be a credible threat to the Union army besieging Vicksburg.

Grant took the threat seriously, and he kept his cavalry busy watching the Big Black River fords for any sign that Johnston was about to cross. One of the units patrolling the river was the 4th Iowa Cavalry, and on June 22, a detachment of 130 men from the regiment were ordered to the Birdsong's Ferry river crossing. The job they were given was to obstruct the road leading to the ferry by felling trees across it.

The Yankees were busy carrying out their orders when they were suddenly attacked by a Confederate combat patrol consisting of Wirt Adams' Mississippi cavalry and the 28th Mississippi Cavalry. The small group of Iowans was forced to make a fighting retreat in the face of the much larger Rebel force, which numbered nearly 1,000 men.

Due to the nature of the terrain, which was heavily forested and cut by deep ravines, the Confederates were forced to charge straight down the

Above: The flag of the 28th Mississippi Cavalry is from the Collections of the Old Court House Museum.

Opposite page: Skirmishers are shown fighting in the dense woods near Vicksburg. (*The Soldier in Our Civil War*)

98

road, and a number of Southern saddles were emptied by the concentrated Yankee fire that swept the roadbed.

Eventually, the Southern advantage in numbers began to tell, and the Federals wcrc forccd to flee to avoid being surrounded and captured. The sharp clash produced 22 Confederate casualties and 24 Union casualties.

On hearing of the fight at Hill's Plantation, Grant moved quickly to counter what he thought was Johnston's first move against the rear of his army. Grant detached almost half his army and sent it east under the command of General Sherman to guard the line of the Big Black River from Johnston's Confederates.

By the time the siege of Vicksburg ended, Sherman's force on the Big Black had grown to 34,000 men and 72 pieces of artillery. Their position was such a strong one that Johnston never made a serious attempt to attack the Yankees, and Grant was able to successfully complete the process of starving the Vicksburg defenders into submission.

PRETTY GIRL, MUSIC WON SOLDIER'S HEART

One of the most interesting events that occurred during the great siege of Vicksburg was the quick courtship and marriage of Captain James P. Burem and Miss Nettie Green.

Captain Burem was a native of Hawkins county, Tennessee, born April 18, 1839. He enlisted as a private in Company G, Thirty-First Tennessee Regiment, but rapidly rose to the rank of Captain. His command was in Vicksburg, and on an early morning in March, while returning to camp from picket duty, with another officer he called at a house on the way, where a young lady was playing "Annie Laurie." He fell in love with the beautiful player at sight, and they were married on April 15th. The wedding was a sensation, and in response to a serenade he made a thrilling speech.

After the capitulation of Vicksburg, Captain Burem called upon General Grant, who graciously gave him permission to take a carriage and servant with his bride through the lines. They visited his home in Hawkins county, where he remained but a short time.

After being exchanged, he reorganized his company, and was soon at the front. Near Piedmont, Virginia, on the ill-fated Sunday of June 5, 1864, he was killed while resisting an assault by the enemy. Captain Burem's body was never recovered, but his father erected a handsome monument to his memory in the family burying ground in his native county.

—Confederate Veteran
July 1895

The Shirley House, also called the White House by the troops, was between the two armies but survived the war, though badly damaged. During the siege, soldiers of the 45th Illinois Infantry built dugouts on the hillside by the house, seeking protection from rain and sun. The house is in the Vicksburg National Military Park. (OCHM)

REBEL WIDOW HAD AN UNLIKELY FRIEND

Josephine Erwin
She saved the flag.

Widowed, in poor health, financially destitute and among strangers—that was the situation in which Josephine Erwin found herself on July 4, 1863, in Vicksburg, but she discovered a friend in someone she would never have expected.

Mrs. Erwin had left her home in Independence, Missouri, when the Yankees took possession; she and her two small daughters came to Vicksburg to be near her husband, Col. Andrew Eugene Erwin, commander of the 6th Missouri Infantry, C. S. A. He was the grandson of Kentucky's famous senator, Henry Clay.

When the defeated Confederates stacked arms at the conclusion of the siege, only eleven men of Company A of the 6th Missouri had survived. Among the dead was Erwin, killed while fighting at the crater only a few days earlier. Before losing his life, he entrusted the battle-torn flag of the regiment to his wife for safekeeping.

Among the survivors of the 6th Missouri was Lt. Erwin A. Hickman, who set about to help the widow. On his way to seek an interview with General Grant concerning Mrs. Erwin's predicament, he met another Missourian, Col. Rob Fletcher, who was on the Union side. Hickman told the story to Fletcher, and together, the two men, one in gray, the other in blue, went to plead Mrs. Erwin's case. The general listened politely and quietly to Hickman's story.

"Where does Mrs. Erwin wish to be sent?" he asked.

"To her late husband's relatives at Lexington, Kentucky," Hickman replied.

Turning to his adjutant, Colonel Rawlings, Grant instructed that Mrs. Erwin and her children be furnished transportation to Lexington and that a guard of honor be detailed to assure her safe conduct.

"Has Mrs. Erwin any money?" Grant asked Hickman.

"She has only a small amount of Confederate money," was the reply.

"Then," Grant said, handing Hickman a $50 greenback, "give her this with my compliments."

Before leaving Vicksburg, Mrs. Erwin met with the Union commander and thanked him for his kindness, though she could not bring herself to shake hands with him.

Beneath her skirts was the flag of the 6th Missouri, which she safely took to Kentucky.

—*Confederate Veteran Magazine*
October 1928

Col. A. E. Erwin
He paid the ultimate price.

Josephine Erwin took the banner of the 6th Missouri with her when she left Vicksburg. Known as the Van Dorn Corps pattern flag, the unusual design was suggested by Gen. Earl Van Dorn, as he wanted a battle flag that would not be easily confused with the Stars and Stripes.

The photographs of the Erwins and the flag are courtesy of Colonel and Mrs. Erwin's great-great-grandson, Wood Simpson, and Kent Masterson Brown of Lexington, Kentucky.

Upon looking up the street I beheld a sight that I fondly hoped never to see. A Yankee officer, in blue uniform, galloping down the streets of Vicksburg. This too on the 4th of July . . . tears of bitter anguish fell from my eyes & a cloud of darkness & gloom settled upon my mind . . . No more shall I roam over those lovely hills & deep valleys, for they are now in possession of a hate-ful foe . . .

—Rev. William Lovelace Foster
Baptist minister and chaplain
35th Mississippi Infantry
July 4, 1863

LAST CASUALTY OCCURRED DURING SURRENDER

The siege of Vicksburg ended on a tragic note, with the last casualty occurring while the surrender was taking place. The victim was Samuel Miller of Company E, 38th Mississippi Infantry. E. W. Thornhill, also of the 38th, wrote that the men had been ordered "to gather up all the loose guns that were lying in the ditches, and stack them up. We had marched eight or ten paces beyond our fortifications and were arranging our guns. Miller was touching me on my right and a man on the right of him. His name I have forgotten. The first gun that Lewis Guy threw up on the fortress was an old musket, loaded with buckshot. The hammer in striking the hard clay caused it to explode and six or seven shot entered Miller between the shoulders, making a slight wound in the flesh. Miller turned around and inquired who did it, and never again uttered a word. He began to fall, and I saw the blood beginning to flow from his mouth. We held him and soon life was extinct. I was one of the detail that helped bury him. He was removed to our side and buried.

—Eleazer W. Thornhill
Company E, 38th Mississippi Infantry
unpublished memoir owned by

At the time of the surrender, Confederate soldiers stacked arms and marched out of their works. Even in defeat, Southern fortifications were not penetrated by the enemy. (*Harper's Weekly*)

Daily Herald.

BY IRA A. BATTERTON.

VICKSBURG, MISS.,
WEDNESDAY, SEPT. 21, 1864.

The Experiment at Davis' Bend.

There is at Davis' Bend a great experiment in progress of what the Freedmen may be expected to do hereafter.—There are about 75 farmers working land on their own account, and making about 1,200 acres of cotton, besides as much more corn.

This trial of their capacity and readiness to work—planned and encouraged by Col. Eaton—is a success. They will make, on an average, from $2,000 to $5,000 each.

There is scarcely one failure among the seventy-five lessees. Some negroes this year will clear from $10,000 to $20,-000, who were *slaves* three years ago. And yet men still wonder "what shall be done with the blacks." There is *one* good use to which they might be put, viz: to instruct those who know no better than to ask such a question now!

Jeff. Davis' plantation is all covered with these negro farms, and just where the rebellion was hatched shall rise up the demonstration that black men need only opportunity to solve the great problem that has so vexed the politicians.

"Ellet's Marine Brigade."

Gen. Canby has done a good thing in mustering out of service the "Marine Brigade." This, says the Boston Post, was Ellet's scheme, and schemes that a visionar signed. In finest river indiscribab the picture land Times house, and w able flotilla ment immens tical good is cent. These bie summer re largely in dema ally where they seldom at hand removal will pro regular river boat our regular army tolerate anything great portion of th of this war is attri chant of volunteer all sorts of experim and if the officer is quarters, his request granted, and person patriotism is unbound the officer and lighten [New Albany Ledger,

DEFENSE OF THE

EDITOR HERALD:—It of indignation and cont rused the above erronous tory article which lately certain unprincipled, non perhead Journal, concernir Mississippi Marine Brigade, and it is for the purpose of refuting the base assertions therein made, that I, an humble member of the said organization, have undertaken the delicate task of vindicating our rights and exhonorating our character; for, allow me the liberty to inform the mendacious Editor and all

ting the grand cause of "putting down the Rebellion." We are not assumed to submit our record of any inspection take the to pass rence is in his ving a Davis bat it cow class. the reof, of eds

what further evidence the rnicious and hypocritical busy-bodies can desire of the integrity and honest in tentions of those in comma Brigade? I am convinced th eral occasions when we have companied by land troops, deeds were maliciously or charged to the "Marines," wh in no wise implicated, and guilty in knowing the facts.

Guerrillas in Henderson, Ky.

THE FARMER'S BANK ROBBED

From the Evansville (Ind.) Journal of the 12th instant, we glean the following:

About 10 o'clock on Saturday Ad Anderson, accompanied by twenty-on other thieves dashed into Henderson taking the people entirely by surpris and at once made a dash for the F mer's B nk, which they robbed of rge amount of money in gold and greenbacks.

From a gentleman of this city, who was in Henderson on Saturday during the raid, and whose relations with that city enables him to obtain correct information, we learn that the amount money stolen by the robbers wa probably over $5,000 or $6,000, t the exact amount could not be tained, as most of the money w special deposit. The Bank only 5270 of its own on hand; most oney being kept in this city.

The front doors of the Bank had t been opened, and the scoundre ed by a side-door, and at once o the vault. Our informant desc m as the meanest looking ves he ever saw.

he effort to pursue the th rove successful, but the in e people of Henderson and we doubt if another d is made on that city by mptible a force.

The Proposed Union of British North American P

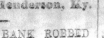

A photograph of Miss Emma Kline and her two Union guards is imposed over a copy of an 1864 Union newspaper. Miss Kline was arrested and imprisoned for her Confederate activities in the Vicksburg area. (Michael J. McAfee)

THE MILITARY OCCUPATION OF VICKSBURG

There is a class of persons in that section
who require watching; although seemingly
disposed to remain quietly at home and pursue
their peaceful avocations, they are hostile in spirit. . . .

—Gen. James B. McPherson
September 27, 1863
in reference to citizens who
lived in the country south
of Vicksburg

With Pemberton's surrender, the war was over for many of the soldiers, but for the citizens of Vicksburg, the horrors they would face were, perhaps, worse than life during the siege. They were literally a people without a country, and they were reminded of that each day by a military commander who had an army at his disposal to enforce his edicts.

For the next two years, the populace enjoyed few freedoms. Property was wantonly destroyed or confiscated, freedom of speech was not permitted, and the necessities of life were doled out at the discretion of the Yankees. Life itself was in constant peril. Lincoln's suspension of the writ of habeas corpus enabled the military to arrest anyone they wished, regardless of charges.

Though it was a bitter pill to swallow, signing the hated loyalty oath to the Federal government and disavowing any Confederate sympathies was sometimes both the wisest and most expedient path to follow, and many no doubt affixed their names to the

III.

Gentlemen May Cry
"Peace, Peace"
When

There Is No Peace

—**Patrick Henry, March 23, 1775**
in his speech before the
Virginia Convention

documents while under duress, though they remained unconquered in sentiment and spirit. Those who refused to sign the oath were often insulted, harassed, and kept under surveillance.

For the slaves, the Fourth of July meant freedom, and most welcomed the Northern soldiers. Monroe Gibson, a slave on the Fortner Plantation at Yokena, was in the field when he heard the news, and he said simply, "I drapt my hoe" and went to Vicksburg. Eventually, over 25,000 black refugees flocked into "Freedom City," all looking to their liberators for sustenance and protection.

There were a number of military commanders of the city—Gens. John A. Logan, James B. McPherson, Henry W. Slocum, Napoleon J. T. Dana, and Morgan L. Smith. Each interpreted the law as it suited him or made new ones. The position was certainly no popularity contest, but McPherson earned the respect of the citizens because of his gentlemanly deportment, and Smith married a Vicksburg girl.

A typical day in occupied Vicksburg must have resembled a modern-day movie scene: grim-faced, well-armed soldiers stand on the corners of the shell-damaged streets; civilians scurry past them looking down, thinking it rash to do anything else.

Residents got their first taste of life under military rule the day of Pemberton's surrender. Before sundown, they watched helplessly while wholesale pillage by Union soldiers, who were joined by some Rebels, began.

"Houses and stores were broken open, and their contents appropriated by the plunderers," Alexander Abrams, a Confederate soldier, wrote. When Gen. U. S. Grant heard of the depredations, he tried to halt the action by placing a regiment on guard "to preserve order and to prevent pillaging and other destruction of property." Victims were urged to make claims of stolen property.

Perhaps it was a conciliatory move when Grant named Gen. John

MAJ. GEN. J. A. LOGAN.

Entered according to Act of Congress, A. D. 1863, by BARR & YOUNG, in the Clerk's Office of the District Court of the U. S. for the So. District of Ohio.

This photograph of Maj. Gen. John A. Logan was taken in Vicksburg after the siege. (OCHM)

A. Logan military governor, for the Illinois officer had been a Vicksburg resident for a brief time when he was a youth. Another order, however, left no doubt in the minds of the public of their future circumstances: former slaves were outfitted as policemen, a move that antagonized the populace.

Though Union officials pretended to frown upon pillaging, they thought nothing of taking residences for personal or military use. Some families were evicted; others were allowed space in the attic. When the siege began, many families fled to the safety of hastily dug caves; others had already sought refuge in the country, and their homes were termed "abandoned" and taken for military housing.

Max Kuner returned to find his home inhabited by Yankees and asked, "By what authority, sir, do you take possession of a man's house?"

"That's none of your damned business," the officer replied. "Who are you?"

"I'm the owner of the house," Kuner replied.

"Are you a loyal citizen?" the Yankee demanded.

"That," the furious Kuner replied, "is none of your damned business." He then went to Grant, who ordered the troops to vacate the house.

Such depredations were widespread. When Aquilla Bowie returned home, he met Union soldiers carrying off all they could, including the Bowies' daughter's wedding dress. On the banks of the Big Black River, Mrs. Sophia Messenger was held prisoner in her own home while soldiers hauled away her possessions by the wagonload.

The victors didn't concentrate on only harassing Confederates. Outspoken Unionists, such as L. S. Houghton, probate judge for the county, and William L. Sharkey, chief justice of the Mississippi Supreme Court, were victims of Union plunder, sanctioned by the army. Mrs. Candis Newman, who owned a dairy on the edge of

Maxmillian Kuner
A German immigrant watchmaker and jeweler. Kuner's home and business were confiscated by Northern troops. (Laurier McDonald)

town, had her cows stolen by Federal soldiers, depriving her of a livelihood. It made no difference that she was a "free woman of color" who was loyal to the Union.

When a small group of tired and weary nuns from the Sisters of Mercy, who had left the city to nurse the sick and wounded in Alabama, tried to return to Vicksburg, they were denied passes. Eventually, permission was granted, but once inside the city, they found that Federal troops occupied their property. All outbuildings had been burned, the grounds ruined, fences destroyed, and the convent in a deplorable state. Only after a direct appeal to Washington were the soldiers evicted and the nuns' quarters returned.

Other religious groups and some individuals were not so fortunate. Invading troops totally demolished the Episcopal church at Bovina and the nearby Methodist church at Mount Alban, east of Vicksburg, and also another Methodist sanctuary near Hankinson's Ferry, south of the city. The Methodist church at Redbone was confiscated and used as a hospital, and barracks were built on the grounds, the lumber taken from nearby plantations. The interior of one city church was described as having "no pews, no altar, no floor. Negroes were living in the church, and they cooked on the remains of the floor. Dishes and bodies were washed in the marble font." All city churches were damaged.

The pastors of the Methodist and Baptist congregations were in other areas of the Confederacy ministering to the needy and to the soldiers and were not allowed to return to the city until after the war ended. Rev. W. W. Lord, the Episcopal minister, was offered safe passage to the North by General Grant, but Lord (who was from New York) chose to cast his lot with the Confederacy, and he and his family left with the paroled troops.

In some instances, fine residences were destroyed, including

This notice in the *Daily Herald* advised citizens that it was illegal to sell gray cloth. (OCHM)

the Lum home, where Grant had lived; Belmont, the Smedes home overlooking the river; the Castle on the edge of the city; and LaGrange, one of the nation's largest orchards, located east of Vicksburg. In most cases, the demolition was one without provocation, without cause.

One of the surrender terms agreed to by Grant had been that the victors would share rations with the soldiers and civilians, and steamboats docking at the wharf on the afternoon of the surrender had lured citizens, both the hungry and the curious, from their homes. Rations were distributed to the paroled Confederate soldiers, but for the civilians, the process of going to the post commissary required visits to a half-dozen or so military offices with paperwork and long waits required at each—all for five days' rations.

When Mrs. Virginia Rockwood applied for rations, General McPherson wrote an order referring to her as a "destitute citizen." The feisty lady advised him to change the wording to "robbed citizen," and amused by her candor, McPherson rewrote the order, doubling the rations. When the list was being filled by a clerk, Mrs. Rockwood indignantly informed the soldier that asking for food did not humiliate her one bit, as she was only getting back "something you have stolen. . . ."

An Illinois private in Company E, 8th Illinois Infantry, Richard R. Puffer, tended to agree with the Rebel lady's assessment. In a letter to his sister on July 22, 1863, he noted that no stores were yet open, and some people came from as far away as twenty miles to draw rations, "having been robed [sic] by one army or the other of all they had."

Those who came represented every segment of society, wrote Sgt. William L. Brown, a cannoneer with the Chicago Mercantile Battery. He figured that most had signed the loyalty oath only so they could receive provisions. Awaiting their turns at the commissary, he wrote,

Civilians were given provisions by the Union army. (Giambrone Collection)

Southern women swallowed their pride and went to the United States Commissary for supplies and food. (*The Soldier in Our Civil War*)

were "men who before the war counted their fortunes by hundreds of thousands, ladies who never before knew the difference between a hind quarter of mutton and a hind quarter of beef, contrabands who have always trembled in the presence of their 'massirs' 'poor white trash,' and last but not least Uncle Sam's own blue uniformed soldiers—all mixed in a heavy mess, trying to be in first to have his or her order filled."

Brown told of one older citizen who had come for food. He was A. B. Reading, former railroad entrepreneur who also owned a large plantation, two cotton gins, and a foundry that made cannon for the Confederacy. Reading had lost it all, but Brown found that "He is an avowed secessionist and does not hesitate to say so." He was typical of many defiant citizens.

A Union physician, Dr. Seneca B. Throll, wrote to his wife that he had seen a rickety old wagon coming down the street, pulled by a poor mule and driven by a little black boy who was "all eyes and teeth." In the wagon bed, sitting on hay, were several women who looked "with proud disdain upon the vulgar Yankees. They formerly rode in a fine carriage, with a negro in livery for a driver, smiling graciously upon their favored admirers," he imagined, but scoffed at "how have the mighty fallen—a rickety wagon, a poor mule, a little ragged nigger."

On occasion Puffer witnessed a similar scene, and his comrade helped a lady off her horse and back again. He described her as "graceful and appeared to be refined and cultivated" and speculated that "some Federal soldier is riding in their carriage."

His assessment was verified by Gen. Cadwallader C. Washburn, who wrote to his daughter, "The people of Vicksburg, before the war, were rich and happy, they had fine houses, fine grounds, elegant furniture and plenty of money, with servants without number. All the country around was occupied by rich plantations, and everybody was, as he supposed, rich and powerful. Now all is changed. Most of the fine houses are occupied by federal officers, their grounds have been devastated and destroyed, many of the inmates are wandering about the country without money to buy a loaf of bread, thousands have perished in the war, and many that remain at their once happy homes, are living on the bounty of our fort."

An example of the despair suffered by the citizens was described in later years by Ida Luckett, recalling what happened to the family farm, which was operated by her widowed grandmother, who was raising the children of her son-in-law who was killed at the Battle of Seven Pines. Mrs. Luckett watched as soldiers herded her cattle down the lane and hitched teams to her farm wagons, piled so high with plunder they creaked as they were driven in gruesome procession toward Vicksburg.

Some of the soldiers made a final sweep of the premises, sparing not so much as a nest egg. As she watched the work of a lifetime wiped away in an afternoon, she sobbed and wrung her hands and then turned and went inside. Destitute and hungry with not enough food for the family, she left most of what she had for the children. The story could be told again and again on farms and plantations all over Warren County.

For civilians, there was virtually no freedom of movement, as a pass was required to either leave or enter town, and a curfew restricted evening meetings, even at a church. A pass was no guarantee that a citizen would not be harassed, as Max Kuner discovered. Guards cursed him and made him dismount and walk a long distance to headquarters. He reflected that he had never mistreated a black person, yet he was subjected to such treatment because he was white.

Grant issued an order calling upon residents to "pursue their peaceful avocations, in obedience to the laws of the United States."

A pass for two Vicksburg ladies to cross the Big Black River was signed by General McPherson. (OCHM)

It was impossible, however, to live a normal life when bands of soldiers were a daily threat. A group of residents of the Oak Ridge community northeast of Vicksburg drafted an appeal for protection, as several citizens along Deer Creek, north of Vicksburg, had been murdered. They sent their petition to Gen. William T. Sherman, whose troops were stationed in the area.

Sherman's reply was a rambling harangue that reasoned "we are justified in treating the inhabitants as combatants" and would be justified in exiling all of them. He called their complaints and fears "little annoyances."

The worst fear was realized on May 18, 1864, when a group of soldiers murdered John H. Bobb after he ordered some soldiers off his property when he found them picking flowers. They cursed him, and he struck one with a brick. Bobb went to headquarters, and reported the incident to Gen. Henry W. Slocum, and on his way home, the soldiers accosted Bobb, took him to a nearby railroad yard, and shot him. Slocum dispatched one of his staff to the scene, and when the officer arrived, Mrs. Bobb was weeping over her husband's body while a throng of soldiers shouted, "We've got them now."

Ira Batterton, a discharged Union soldier who edited the *Vicksburg Daily Herald,* feared for the "security of life to any man" and thought Slocum "unfit for command" if the guilty were not arrested and hanged. One soldier did stand trial, but he was acquitted.

The next winter, several residents of Issaquena County, north of Vicksburg, were murdered by deserters from the Union army. On March 17, 1865, Simeon B. Cook was killed near Vicksburg; no arrests were made. Two weeks later, Union troops raided the home of Jared Reese Cook, east of the city, where they seriously wounded him and murdered Mrs. Cook. Gen. Napoleon Dana, commander of the city, offered a $500 reward; three soldiers turned state's evidence, and nine others were hanged for the murder.

Slaves at Vicksburg enjoying a New Year's dance in the 1860s (*Frank Leslie's Illustrated*)

Stories about attacks by Confederates unnerved carpetbaggers like Isaac Shoemaker, who had come from Ohio and leased a plantation south of Vicksburg. He wrote that he found it difficult to sleep because of the anxiety. One night, soon after retiring, he heard the firing of two rifles in the slave quarters. In a flash, he was at the kitchen window, "and my heart fairly jumped to my mouth as I heard what sounded exactly like the galloping of horsemen coming near; I ran back, put on my trousers, & then again to the window." Gradually, the terrified man realized that the sound of horse hooves drew no closer. It wasn't the Confederates at all—it was the servants, down in the quarters, having a dance, their heavy shoes sounding like galloping horses.

Though Batterton occasionally criticized military authorities, the general public dared not do the same. Some were arrested for "disrespectful language to the Government of the United States." In most cases, the exact comments are unknown, though the provost marshal's records report that E. A. Hornish was arrested for stating he "wished to God [Gen. Nathan B.] Forest would come and kill ever yank in Vicks[burg]," and Nathan Renwick was charged with "cheering for Jeff Davis in the streets of Vicksburg."

For five Vicksburg ladies, their actions were as loud as words: they were banished from Vicksburg for walking out of Christ Church when the minister prayed for Abraham Lincoln rather than Jefferson Davis. On another occasion, Mrs. Elizabeth Eggleston was sent to "Rebeldom" (territory on the east side of the Big Black River, held by the Confederates) because of charitable deeds she performed for civilian prisoners.

In the winter of 1864, General McPherson exiled the Nineon E. Kline family, accusing them of "acting in bad faith" toward the government. He allowed them to take what personal property they could; the rest was turned over to the government. McPherson was suspicious of most of those who lived near the Klines, stating they "require watching; although seemingly disposed to remain quietly at home and pursue their peaceful avocations, they are hostile in spirit. . . ."

When Unionists were expelled from Yazoo and Hinds counties by Confederate authorities, homes of die-hard Vicksburg Rebels were confiscated for their use. Several who had refused to sign the loyalty oath were fined by military authorities and the money given to the new residents, the unrepentant Southerners, including such prominent men as Richard Barnett, judge, and Dr. William T. Balfour, each of whom was assessed $250. On another occasion, twenty-two citizens from nearby Port Gibson were arrested and

Pickets checked passes for both whites and blacks in the Confederacy, and the Union continued and tightened travel restrictions during occupation. Almost every activity required a pass or permit. (*The Civil War in the United States*)

[See page 120.]

HE PRAYED FOR LINCOLN

Rev. James Angel Fox (OCHM)

Though it was a season of peace on Earth, the truce between Yankee occupation forces and the defiant Rebels was a fragile one when they assembled for worship at Christ Episcopal Church in Vicksburg on Christmas day in 1863.

Six months earlier, worshipers had braved almost continuous shelling to attend daily prayers in the rubble-littered sanctuary. After the surrender, the congregation was left without a pastor when Rev. W. W. Lord, though a New York native, chose to go with the Confederate army.

As the Christmas season approached, a Union official asked Rev. James Angel Fox, a retired Episcopal minister who lived east of town, to conduct services. Though from Connecticut, he had lived in Mississippi almost half a century. He was affectionately called "Parson Fox."

A Unionist, Fox had four sons in the Confederate army—so he possibly had mixed emotions about the prayer in the Episcopal service for the president. Perhaps, he could just omit it, praying for neither President Davis nor President Lincoln—but the commander of the occupation forces said otherwise.

As the worship service began, Parson Fox noted several Vicksburg ladies seated near the front of the church; he turned and met the cold and daring stare of several Union officers. With a sigh, he prayed that the Lord would "behold and bless thy servant, the President of the United States . . ."

There was a stir, then Mrs. Moore, wife of a vestryman of the church, and Kate and Ellen Barnett, Laura Latham, and Ellen Martin stood, drew themselves to their full height, and, with a swishing of skirts and an angry tapping of feet, marched the full length of the aisle, past the blue uniforms and out into the cold morning air.

Consequences were swift. Gen. James B. McPherson accused them of acting "disrespectfully toward the President of the United States" and ordered them banished within forty-eight hours to Confederate territory or go to jail. He warned that in the future anyone who "by word, deed or implication, do insult or show disrespect to the President, the government or the Flag . . . shall be fined, banished, or imprisoned. . . ."

But what of Parson Fox? A close friend and stalwart Confederate, Mahala Roach, said in 1874, "Many citizens ever since have not treated Mr. Fox in the same social manner that they did before this occurrence."

Above: An official Episcopal prayer specifically names the Confederate States of America. This one belonged to Reverend Fontaine. (OCHM)

Left: Christ Church as it appeared in the late 1800s (OCHM)

"EVERY CLASS OF CRIMINALS KNOWN TO THE CALENDAR OF CRIME"

"When we were halted in front of the jail, I heard a cry of 'fresh fish' proceeding from many of the inmates of the prison, a rather pleasing sound to our half-starved crowd, but we soon learned that we were the fresh fish, and that this was the mode of announcing the arrival of new prisoners. We were carefully searched before going in and. . . . were thrust in amidst new and more vociferous cries of fresh fish, by which cries all the prisoners not closely confined were attracted, and we were for the time 'a gazing stock' to one of the motliest crowds of humanity ever assembled together, speaking as many tongues almost at the 'devout Jews' who were assembled at Jerusalem on the days of Pentecost.

"The prisoners numbered some three hundred, representing Federal and Confederate soldiers and civilians, common thieves, highway robbers, murderers, blockade runners—in fact every class of criminals known to the calendar of crime. There was in the crowd young men and old men, boys, a few white women, and a number of negroes. It was was indeed a grand medley of humanity with dark secrets locked up in many a breast. . . . It was a relief to find amongst the civilian prisoners a number of old friends. . . . They doubtless saved me from becoming a victim to an outrage practiced by some of the 'baser sort' of prisoners. . . . They got me into their mess and found lodging for me in the cell occupied by themselves at night. They were locked up at night at their own request to save them from the thieves and murderers in the crowd. Fourteen of us occupied the cell at night, and we had control of it by day. We would lie down seven on a side, with our feet touching and each man with any weapon he had or could procure under his head, as a protection against the robbers and murderers should they break down our door. We were suspected of having money, and our clothes, though not fine, were good enough to be coveted by those wretches. We were careful not to move about by day or night.

The Warren County jail at the corner of Cherry and Grove streets was photographed about 1864 from the courthouse roof. The jail was used by Confederates and then by the Federals. (OCHM)

"There was scarcely a day that the cry of 'fresh fish' was not heard . . . I saw them from our window one day 'go for' a fancy colored barber of the city, who was committed for some petty misdemeanor. He was the very 'class of fashion' upon entering, but in a few minutes he looked and doubtless felt like a live chicken stripped of its feathers. He came out of his Wellington boots into his stocking feet, and from under his stove-pipe hat quicker that I can tell the story. These things were done with the knowledge of the officers.

"The most pitable sight in the prison, perhaps, was the few old men who had been ruthlessly torn from their homes and made to walk long distances, arrested upon some shallow pretense or to gratify some private grudge or spite. The witnesses against them could never be found, and they were without friends to represent them at headquarters. They languished in prison for months, some of them, uncared for, and were finally released without trial. There were also lads of very tender years in the crowd. Neither they, nor anyone else knew why they were arrested. But such is war:

The inhumanity of man to man
Makes countless thousands mourn."

—Horace S. Fulkerson
A Civilian's Recollections of the
War Between the States

Members of the First Mississippi Colored Cavalry escort captured Confederates to the Vicksburg jail in 1864. (*Frank Leslie's Illustrated*)

Occupation forces constructed earthworks along what appears to be South and Cherry streets in 1864. In the distance are the steeples of St. Paul Catholic Church, Crawford St. Methodist Church, and the cupola of the courthouse. *(Frank Leslie's Illustrated)*

Barricades, such as this one on Washington Street at the intersection with China, were constructed by occupation troops just in case of a Confederate attack. (OCHM)

jailed in Vicksburg "to be held as hostages." This group included five women and one twelve-year-old boy.

Though some women made no efforts to conceal their disdain for the Northerners, others sought to ingratiate themselves, and, according to Alice Shannon, "seem to be turning blue" and attended social functions hosted by wives of Federal officers and went to dances with Yankee soldiers. There were even a few North-South weddings.

Some who had been quietly pro-Union now openly expressed their sentiments. When Abraham Lincoln was reelected in 1864, a leader among the local Unionists joined occupation forces in staging a celebration. A Union League was formed, and money was collected to assist programs of the Northern government. One group of Vicksburg Unionists, upon hearing of the death of Lincoln, met and passed resolutions of sorrow and respect, approved by some but much to the disgust of others.

The main prison used by the occupation forces was the county jail. In addition to a two-story brick building surrounded by a high wall, there were two large metal cages in the yard, a wooden building, and another structure for women. Prisoners slept on the floor, and fare was usually bean soup and other unpalatable food. If one had money, he could purchase better food from the jailer; friends would sometimes bring food and clothing. The arrival of prisoners, especially captured Confederate soldiers, was announced by an army band and guards escorting them down the street through lines of curious onlookers.

White citizens were a small problem numerically when compared to the crowds of blacks who came into town. A Union soldier described a typical procession: "Such a sight as met my gaze. All along the road were negroes with their families, household goods, everything they could gather in the short time, piled up in their immense cotton wagons as high as they could get them. There must have been thousands, no end to the children; 'going to freedom'. . . .

They sang and danced, kissed each other and all the extravagant demonstrations of joy you can imagine were carried on."

Their lot was often pathetic, and thousands died from the squalor in which they lived and diseases that infested their makeshift camps. Such hordes were a real encumbrance to the military, but official Lincoln policy directed the army to encourage the blacks to come into the Union lines, though both Grant and Sherman were opposed, especially when some were inducted into the service. To ease friction, officials formed blacks into segregated regiments commanded by whites. In addition, farms and camps were established for the freedmen. Appeals were made in the North for help, and missionaries came to set up schools and operate the Sanitary Commission for the former slaves.

Henry Rountree and his wife, missionaries from Indiana, discovered the camp at Young's Point appalling, for several thousand people were living in filth. The same situation was found at Ursino Plantation at Davis Bend, where huddled together in a cow shed were "poor wretchedly helpless negroes, one man who had lost one eye entirely, and the sight of the other fast going. . . . They had no bedding, two old quilts, and a soldier's old worn out blanket comprised the whole for 35 human beings." At other places freedmen lived in hovels made of branches, brush, and sod.

The situation was equally bad in the city, where many lived in dirty, rundown shacks and lean-tos near the river; many had no shelter at all. Rent was high—$20 a month for a room—and few blacks or whites had that much money. They continued to arrive by the score, thousands following Sherman's army across the state from Meridian. Sherman guessed that the line was ten miles long. They came—all ages, sexes, and conditions—the editor of the Herald wrote—riding in conveyances ranging from a "nice family carriage to a Negro cart—all filled with children and the hopelessly

Alice Shannon
She hated the color blue. (OCHM)

121

Left: Capt. Isaac R. Whitaker headed an independent command, Whitaker's Scouts, who waged guerilla warfare near Vicksburg. (OCHM)

Below: Union cavalry and Whitaker's Scouts clash in a skirmish near Redbone Church, south of Vicksburg in 1864. *(Frank Leslie's Illustrated)*

122

infirm of both sexes. . . . In one wagon I counted thirty four children. . . . crying and chattering like so many monkees." Local residents, such as Alice Shannon, who wrote "I can't help feeling sorry for them," could do nothing, as they were also impoverished as a result of the war. Federal agencies argued over who was responsible.

Another problem was what to do about the abandoned plantations. One plan was to confiscate them, lease them to loyal speculators who would in turn hire former slaves to plant, work, and harvest cotton, which would be shipped to Northern mills. Growing or selling cotton was the most lucrative of contraband trade, for every bale was an object of speculation and greed, and permits and leases were coveted. Speculators leased 136 plantations in the Vicksburg area.

Leasing a plantation was easy, but operating it successfully, especially among hostile neighbors, was not. In addition to procuring workers and supplies and abiding by government regulations, the lessees had to contend with Rebel guerillas, who were intent on driving them off the land—or worse.

Corruption was not confined to the Northern civilians, for army officers often cloaked raids as military operations when the objectives were finding and stealing cotton and sending it north under the guise of confiscated Confederate property. It was easy for an officer and a few of his men to pass through the lines on a "raid" and make deals for buying cotton that Southern planters had raised and stored, hoping for the day when it could be sold. It was said that as many as 500 bales passed through Vicksburg each day in March 1864.

General Dana determined to put a stop to the cotton corruption. He levied a $5 tax on each bale brought in by the small boats, which he called "cotton thieves," and attempted to halt all trade with the Confederacy, allowing nothing to be brought across the lines except the personal property of bona-fide refugees.

Inside the city, Dana closed all businesses, fixed a ceiling on the

Here we saw the ordinance trophies of the surrender of Vicksburg. . . . We then visited the yard in which are piled over one hundred thousand cannon balls, shot and shell, of different kinds.

—*Vicksburg Daily Herald*
July 7, 1864 (OCHM)

123

price of saleable items, and ordered that "none but loyal persons shall enjoy the privilege of trade. . . ." With the stroke of a pen, he forced everyone out of business and then selected former Union soldiers, carpetbaggers, a few scalawags, and selected friends as the new merchants of the city. Under the iron will and whims of Dana, Vicksburg residents discovered just how much they were at the mercy of military rulers. He ordered civilians tried in military courts and even forbade the selling of gray cloth. No one was allowed to correspond with relatives or friends in Confederate-held territory.

In further efforts to enforce the loyalty of the people, Dana decreed that only those who had signed an oath of allegiance could hold jobs, buy goods, operate businesses, or have a pass to go in and out of the city. "Disloyal" residents were held financially responsible for any losses incurred from raids on plantations leased by Northerners. It was almost impossible for rural citizens to grow a garden, for the government confiscated all work animals, and every male between the ages of eighteen and forty-five was forced to join the militia.

Guards were provided to protect some families from marauders, and Dana tackled the jobs of street repairs and sanitation with strict rules and action. Crime was greatly curtailed, and Dana was stern with his own men, prescribing severe punishment for many disorderly and disobedient soldiers.

From the time of the surrender of Vicksburg until the close of the war, almost two years later, citizens were subject to martial law, enforced according to the likes and dislikes of the commanding general. When the war ended, occupation did not, for Congress kept the South under military rule, though to a lesser and lesser extent as time passed, for more than a decade, ending with the administration of Pres. Rutherford B. Hayes.

For many in Vicksburg, military occupation had been as bad as, if not worse than, war.

Union troops used various tactics to persuade Southerners to sign the Oath of Allegiance. This one is dated October 27, 1863. (OCHM)

VICTORS CELEBRATED JULY 4 AT BRIERFIELD

The "Freedmen's Paradise" was the way the Union-owned *Vicksburg Daily Herald* described Brierfield Plantation in its July 6, 1864, edition. Earlier in the year, Maj. Gen. Napoleon J. T. Dana had decreed the plantation, several miles south of the city and the home of Confederate president Jefferson Davis, to be a haven for thousands of former slaves, writing that it would be a fitting headquarters "for the unfortunate race he is being so instrumental in oppressing."

A month before the first anniversary of the fall of Vicksburg, editor Ira Batterton of the *Herald* called for a big July 4 celebration in the city, but the main event took place instead at Brierfield.

Early on the morning of the fourth, the steamboat *Diligent* left the Vicksburg wharf loaded with Northern schoolteachers, missionaries, social workers, and U.S. Army personnel. Their destination was Davis Bend. Capt. Henry S. Clubb wrote an account of the celebration for the newspaper.

When the *Diligent* arrived at Hurricane Plantation at Davis Bend, buggies, wagons, and army ambulances were waiting to take the guests to nearby Brierfield. The reporter noted that Joseph Davis's "fine brick house . . . is nearly demolished, but the cottage used as sort of law library and office is remaining uninjured. The negro quarters also remain." He failed to tell that the two-and-one-half-story mansion, owned by the president's older brother, had been wantonly burned by Union soldiers in 1862.

Captain Clubb wrote that "the Jeff Place" was also a very fine plantation but that it remained intact "uninjured except for the door locks and one or two marble mantels broken up, apparently for trophies," and that all the Davis furniture had been stolen.

For the fourth, Brierfield had been decorated by Miss Lee of Pennsylvania and Miss Huddleston of Indiana, who had carried out a theme of "wit and satire for traitors and a cordial welcome for the loyal

. . . this site, from being the home of traitors and oppressors of the poor, had become a sort of earthly paradise for colored refugees. There they flock in large numbers, and like Lazarus of old are permitted, as it were, to "repose in Father Abraham's bosom." The rich men of the "Southern Confederacy," now homeless wanderers, occasionally cry across for the Lazarus whom they have oppressed and despised. . . .

—*Vicksburg Daily Herald*
July 6, 1864 (OCHM)

and patriotic." The two "whole-souled missionaries," hired by the government to teach ex-slaves, had draped flags and bunting around the grounds, and there were flowers and evergreens in the house. Over the front entrance, they had placed a sign made of cedar boughs that read, "The House Jeff Built," and at the rear was another that proclaimed, "Exit Traitor."

Festivities of the day began on the lawn with a Northern missionary opening the program with prayer, another reading the Declaration of Independence, and still another delivering an oration. They then adjourned for a picnic dinner.

An unexpected shower forced the revelers inside the house, and after the repast, the customary toasts—fourteen of them—were proposed and songs were sung. Then the guests talked about freedom and described their absent "host" and other Southern planters as "thieves, murderers, and traitors."

Written especially for the occasion was a song, "The House That Jeff Built," and it was decided a copy be sent to the *New York Tribune* and also to the Confederate president, whose home had been desecrated that day.

During the Brierfield visit, Captain Clubb said he had enjoyed the beauty of the setting and thought about how the slaves had been brought "out from the House of Bondage by the 'God of Abraham'" and that "the very house now occupied by missionaries and teachers had but a year ago, been in the service of despotism; built in fact as a temple of slavery by the great chief who preferred to rule in a miserable petty despotism, to serving in a great and magnanimous Republic. . . ."

The reporter added that Brierfield was now the "Freedmen's Paradise," where the blacks were cultivating the land, protected by the U.S. Army, and were under the direct supervision of Northern missionaries. Instead of working for their former Southern masters, the ex-slaves were making crops for the U.S. government.

When the *Diligent* and its party arrived back in Vicksburg at the end of the day, it was almost midnight. The Fourth had been a memorable

Varina Ann Howell Davis
The South's First Lady
(Library of Congress)

In 1866 Mrs. Jefferson Davis visited Vicksburg but did not go to Brierfield as the Freedman's Bureau was in charge and had strangers living in her house. Many of her former servants called on her, all "respectful and friendly." She gave $20 to provide for the needs of 100-year-old Uncle Bob, who had been robbed by the Yankees.

The situation in Vicksburg was much worse than Jefferson Davis had thought. His wife told him that former slaves "have almost taken Vicksburg — they swarm — but they toil not, neither do they spin."

—Hudson Strode
in *Jefferson Davis: Tragic Hero*

one—a pleasant river trip, patriotic activities, abundant food, pretty decorations, and black soldiers to guard the all-white Northern party who celebrated the "Freedmen's Paradise."

A sign, "The House Jeff Built," was placed over the porch of Brierfield during a Union celebration on July 4, 1864. (OCHM)

Right: Union troops appear on the lawn of the courthouse following the surrender. (OCHM)

Below: Soldiers thought to be members of the 45th Illinois Infantry posed for this group photo on the lawn of the courthouse, probably in 1863. (*Civil War Times*)

HUNDREDS DIED WITH SINKING OF *SULTANA*

They thought they were going home at last, going home after wasting away in prisoner-of-war camps. It was April 1865 and the war was coming to a close. An exchange of prisoners had begun in the winter, and the blue-clad boys were brought from the compounds in Alabama and Georgia to the Big Black River, then transported by trains to Camp Fisk at Four Mile Bridge east of town. After the paperwork was finished, they made the last trip into Vicksburg, then a weary trek from the station to the wharf, where steamboats were waiting.

For many, that walk along the Vicksburg waterfront would be a death march.

Several steamboat captains vied for the job to transport the men. The government was providing the tickets, and there was money to be made. There was an undercurrent of talk that some deals had been cut, and later accusations would be made, though never proved, but for whatever reason, all 1,886 men were placed aboard one boat, along with about 500 other passengers and crew.

The steamboat *Sultana* was a handsome vessel, the third to bear the name. She had been built two years earlier and had become a familiar sight on the river. She had carried the news of Lincoln's murder along with that of Lee's surrender; now, a week later, she would have the privilege of taking the former prisoners home. Over 2,500 people were on board the boat, which had been designed to hold 376. There was little room to sleep; most had to sit and stand on the open decks—but they didn't care—they just wanted to go home.

The crowded boat steamed out of Vicksburg; other vessels remained idle and empty at the wharf. The *Sultana* made stops at Helena and Memphis, heading upriver from the Tennessee city late on April 26. Ominous signs had been seen in the sky before it became excessively dark. A storm was brewing, clouds were gathering, and in the midst of lightning and thunder, violent winds and torrential rains, an explosion

When the *Sultana* burned and sank near Memphis in 1865, it was one of the worst maritime disasters in American history. *(Harper's Weekly)*

Above: A soldier stands guard at Camp Fisk, where released prisoners were housed until they could be exchanged and sent home. (OCHM)

Left: A railroad trestle crossed a ravine four miles east of Vicksburg, giving the location the name Four Mile Bridge. In the background are tents for the guards of Camp Fisk. (OCHM)

with the force of a volcano erupting shook the willows and cottonwoods along the shore, and a hideous glare illuminated the sky as flames, engulfing the steamboat, shot into the air.

Over 1,500 people died in the early morning hours in either the fire or the murky waters; over 1,200 of them were veterans. It was one of the worst maritime disasters in American history.

The last exchange of prisoners at Camp Fisk was held several months after the war ended, but the Confederate officials were allowed to continue to wear their uniforms. Col. H. A. M. Henderson is seated at the table, on the right, and Col. N. G. Watts is standing beside him. Others are not identified. *(Review of Reviews)*

The house was appropriately called the 'Castle' and was complete with towers and turrets and a moat.

Army tents were pitched on the lawn of the Castle. (OCHM)

THE CASTLE

If houses counted their relationships the way people do, there was no better-connected home in Vicksburg than the Castle. It was built in the early 1840s by Thomas E. Robins, who married Jefferson Davis's niece Caroline; later it was bought by Eilbeck Mason, a descendant of Samuel Mason, author of the Virginia Declaration of Rights. Eilbeck Mason's sister married Smith Lee, who was Gen. Robert E. Lee's brother, and his brother James Mason was a Confederate diplomat whose capture on the high seas by a Yankee captain caused an international incident that almost brought England into the war.

The Castle stood on a high hill overlooking the Mississippi River on the south edge of Vicksburg. The house was complete with towers and turrets and a moat, just like an ancient European castle. The terraced hill was planted with seventeen acres of exotic flora. Just before the war began, Mason sold the home to Armistead Burwell, an attorney described as a "broadsword tongued Unionist," who fled to the North after the war started.

The hill was fortified by the Confederates during the siege, and some months after the surrender, the home was destroyed by occupation troops and powerful guns mounted on the site, which the Yankees called Fort Castle. In the 1880s a standpipe for the city's water supply was constructed there, and today the terraced site is still called Castle Hill.

It seems strangely unjust that the home of an outspoken Unionist was destroyed by Union forces—and without provocation.

After the house was destroyed, the hill was leveled and cannons put in place, aimed toward the river. The site was called Fort Castle or the Castle Battery. Burwell not only lost his home, but the Yankees also confiscated from him 135 hogsheads and 14 boxes of sugar, valued at $35,150. In 1879 his widow, Priscilla, received $11,248 from the U.S. government for the loss of the sugar. (OCHM)

Above: The U.S. Mississippi Marine Brigade barracks at Vicksburg in 1864 housed troops who were a mobile force that could be quickly moved up and down the river. They were headquartered in Vicksburg and commanded by Gen. Alfred W. Ellet. (U.S. Army Military History Institute)

Right: The McPherson Hospital was built as a home by A. B. Reading, but by the time of the siege, it had become the city hospital. *(Review of Reviews)*

Above: The railroad yards at Vicksburg in 1864 (Library of Congress)

Left: These five locomotives were built at Vicksburg by Federal soldiers under the supervision of Colonel Coolbaugh of General McPherson's staff. (*Frank Leslie's Illustrated*)

BLACK SOLDIERS SERVED AT VICKSBURG

It is ironic, to some, that the only African Americans who participated in the siege of Vicksburg were wearing Confederate gray. They acted in a variety of roles—usually as cooks, laborers, or teamsters—though a few saw combat or so said the Northern press and some Rebel diaries.

Across the river, at Milliken's Bend, black soldiers on the Union side showed their detractors they could fight, and fight well, when they beat back an attack by the Rebels on June 7, 1863, which included some vicious hand-to-hand combat.

Following the surrender, black troops were used to police the city; many eagerly joined the army, barracks were built to garrison them, and they were organized into regiments commanded by white officers.

The outfitting of former slaves as soldiers was viewed by most local residents as an attempt by the Yankees to further humiliate them in defeat.

Pvt. Andrew Mitchell of Vicksburg was a member of Company B, 50th United States Colored Infantry. He was one of thousands of former slaves who joined the Union army. Mitchell is shown here in later life, wearing his Grand Army of the Republic hat and lapel pin. (OCHM)

Above: A company of United States colored troops standing in formation at Vicksburg to be photographed, probably in 1864 (OCHM)

Right: Colored soldiers at Vicksburg being disciplined by "riding the sawbuck," which was a plank six inches wide. They were forced to remain there for several hours. *(Review of Reviews)*

Opposite page: The barracks at Vicksburg of the 5th United States Colored Heavy Artillery *(Review of Reviews)*

Above: Figures of Union soldiers are blurred as they cross Jackson Street near Openwood, probably in 1864. In the background is the Constitution Engine Firehouse. (Library of Congress)

Left: Gen. John A. Logan, standing fifth from the right, and his staff were photographed in Vicksburg in July 1863. The exact location is unknown. Logan served as the first military governor of the city, appointed by Grant. *(Review of Reviews)*

Top: The Balfour House on Crawford Street was the headquarters for Gen. James B. McPherson following the surrender. Mrs. Balfour and the children moved to Alabama for safety, but Dr. Balfour remained in the city to care for the sick. (Library of Congress)

Bottom: Gen. James B. McPherson (seated wearing a Hardee Hat) and his staff were photographed in the backyard of the Balfour House in 1863. Those identified are from the left: standing and seated, Linessely (Yous)ke (?), unidentified, Ira K. Knox, G. R. Fitch, unidentified, unidentified, General McPherson, W. E. Strong, Capt. John S. Foster (who was part of McPherson's cavalry escort), Bvt. Col. and Aide De Camp William McWherry, and unidentified. (OCHM)

Names	Co	Regt	Oct 2nd 1864 By Whom confined	Charges
L. D. Evans	✓	Cit	By order of Maj' Genl Dana	To be held as hostages
S. Forbes	✓	"		
Edwin Snodgrass	✓	"		
Mrs J Coleman		"		
John M. Parker	✓		"	
Eq A. H. Peck	✓		"	
Jas A Gage	✓		"	
C. C. Perkins			"	
Wilson Watson	✓		"	
D. J. Dorn	✓		"	
F. H. Snodgrass	✓		"	
H. T. Ellett			"	
Eq R. G. Martin	✓		"	
D. G. Link			"	
Mr G. G. Butler	✓		"	
James A McGlaughlin Prij	✓	19th Ark		
Mrs H. T. Ellett		Cit		

A WHITE HOUSE CONNECTION

John M. Parker

"To be held as hostages by the United States Government" is the charge written in the record book of the provost marshal. Twenty citizens of Claiborne County were arrested in the fall of 1864 and placed in the Warren County jail on orders of Gen. Napoleon J. T. Dana. The group included several women and children, one adolescent boy, and more than a dozen men, all from prominent families. Their only offence was that they were Southerners who lived in an area controlled by the enemy army. One of the men was John Milliken Parker; he was released several weeks later, no charges ever having been lodged against him. Parker's father, James, and Eliza Todd were brother and sister—the prisoner was a first cousin to the woman in the White House, Mary Todd Lincoln.

Capt. Alexander Todd

A native of Kentucky, Capt. Alexander Todd served with Confederate forces in Vicksburg in the summer of 1862 as an aide to his brother-in-law, Gen. Benjamin Hardin Helm. Leaving Vicksburg to fight at Baton Rouge, Todd had just completed a letter to his mother when, on August 4, 1862, he was struck and killed by a stray bullet. His sister lived in Washington—she was Mary Todd Lincoln.

Sgt. David Todd

A sergeant in the 27th Louisiana Infantry, David Todd saw service in Vicksburg in 1862 and 1863. He was one of the Confederate soldiers considered to be a prisoner of war when Pemberton surrendered to Grant on July 4, 1863, and was paroled several days later. It is not known if his captors (or his comrades) ever knew that Mary Lincoln was his sister.

VICKSBURG SISTERS SEND GENERAL LEE A GIFT

Was Robert E. Lee wearing a pair of Vicksburg boots when he met with U. S. Grant at Appomattox in 1865? He very well may have been, for two local ladies had sent him boots as a birthday present just a short time before.

The sisters, Sallie and Lucy Marshall, were refugees living in Columbus, Georgia, at the time; they were the daughters of the Reverend Charles K. Marshall of Vicksburg, a Methodist minister who was active in support of the Confederacy. The young ladies were descendants of Vicksburg's founder, the Reverend Newit Vick, through their mother, Amanda Vick Marshall.

On January 8, 1865, a few days before his birthday, Lee wrote the Marshall girls, "I have rec'd the overboots sent me by your father and had the opportunity yesterday of testing their value. It was one of the most tempestuous days of the winter, hail, rain, and sleet. By their means through out all day I was very comfortable. Please accept my grateful thanks for your kindness and believe me with great respect, R. E. Lee."

The boots had been paid for with money carefully saved by Sallie Marshall; she had covered gold pieces and used them as buttons to keep them from being stolen, and some of her "buttons" had been sacrificed to pay for the boots.

When Lee prepared to meet Grant to talk surrender terms, he put on his best apparel—a handsome new uniform, his dress sword, and his deep-red sash, for he expected to become a prisoner of General Grant. He commented, "I must make my best appearance."

His uniform immaculate, his boots well polished—what a contrast Lee was to Grant when the two met, for the Union commander wore a crumpled uniform and mud-spattered boots. A witness of the meeting described Lee as "six feet tall, hair and beard of silver gray, a handsome uniform of Confederate gray buttoned to the throat, with three stars on each side of the turned-down collar, fine topboots with handsome spurs and a splendid sword."

Those fine top boots! Were they the ones from the Vicksburg sisters?

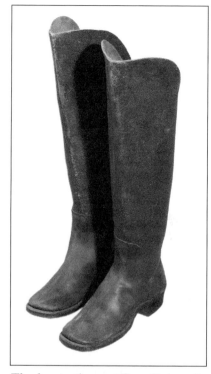

The boots given to Gen. Robert E. Lee probably resembled these Confederate officers' boots from the Old Court House Museum collection.

Right: A view of the Big Black River crossing near Bovina, taken by a Union army photographer, probably in 1864. Yankees called the Confederate territory on the east side of the river "Rebeldom." (Library of Congress)

Below: Pontoon bridges replaced the railroad trestle at Bovina, east of Vicksburg. (OCHM)

Union troops were stationed along the Big Black River in 1863 to guard against possible Confederate attack by Gen. Joseph E. Johnston. They continued to occupy the area until the end of the war. This photo was taken at the crossing near Bovina, probably in 1864. Note the railroad cars and track on the slope to the right. Prisoners of war were picked up here and transported to Four Mile Bridge near Vicksburg for exchange in 1865. (Library of Congress)

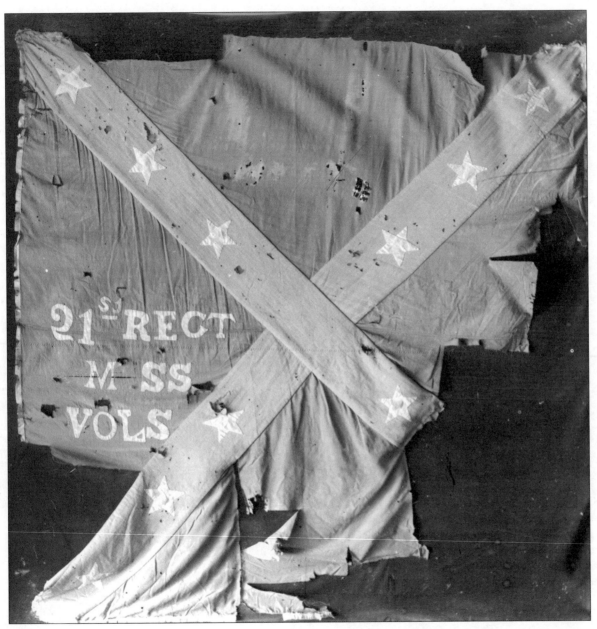

The "flag that never surrendered" is in the collections of the Old Court House Museum.

SOUTHRONS FOUGHT UNTIL THE END, BROUGHT FLAG HOME

Only six men from the Volunteer Southrons, Company A of the 21st Mississippi Infantry, answered the last roll call at Appomattox Court House on April 9, 1865. They were all who remained of the 143 men who had served in the company since it left Vicksburg four years earlier to become a part of the Army of Northern Virginia; they were one of the first units from Mississippi to be mustered into the service of the Confederate States.

Their battle honors were many; they fought in over a dozen major battles and in skirmishes too numerous to count. On the second day at Gettysburg, they advanced the crimson battle flag further than any other Southern banner in the bloody Peach Orchard.

It was at Sayler's Creek, Virginia, only three days before Lee met Grant to surrender the Army of Northern Virginia, that two of the men from the Volunteer Southrons were captured; they were Austin A. Trescott and John M. Collier.

The pair had the regimental flag, which one of them wrapped around his waist beneath his shirt. After a short stay in a prisoner-of-war camp, they were soon on their way home, the flag safe and secure. At some point after they returned to Vicksburg, many of the men who had fought beneath its colors cut pieces from its folds to keep as sacred souvenirs.

Hallowed in battle, untouched by the enemy, the flag of the 21st Mississippi Infantry was never surrendered.

Veterans of the Volunteer Southrons posed with their flag, probably in 1866, in this photo taken by Herrick and Dirr of Vicksburg. Only two men are identified: John M. Collier is seated (left), and Austin A. Trescott is standing (center). (OCHM)

MORE HISTORY.
July 4 1874
Reminiscences of the Siege and
Surrender of Vicksburg.

Under the headline of "The For...
and a Recollection," the Vicksbur...
yesterday had the following:

The glorious Fourth of July will b...
ushered in this morning, but it is likely
to fall upon the public ear about Vicksburg like the recollection of an unpleas-
ant dream.   At this hour (9 p.m.) elev-
en years ago, the city was comparatively silent, though armies confronted
each other from the Warrenton road t...
...Negotiations fo...

VICKSBURG'S
CARNIVAL of the CONFEDERACY
1776
1863
1947

July
3-4-5

**Vicksburg's July 4
Features Modern War**

'Hill City' Makes Up
For 80-Year Silence

Vicksburg, Miss., June 28—The
first city-wide celebration of July
4 in Vicksburg, strategically important city to the Confederate
armies, which fell to the enemy on
July 4, 1863, will be observed
Wednesday with a colossal
a baseball gam...
by the ...
tation fr...
enormous...
things.
B-29's f...
fighter esc...
burg in ...
cording to ...
mand at T...
forts, on t...
be under t...
Col. John ...
distinction o...
flyer who bo...
yo. All the n...
combat fliers
action in the
P-51s will be
of Capt. Dunc...

**Time Heals Old Civil War Wounds
At Vicksburg—Town to Celebrate**

Vicksburg. July 3—(P)—July
Fourth is Independence Day in
Vicksburg, the same as it is everywhere else that Old Glory flies.
The fact that Vicksburg's Confederate defenders surrendered
to General U. S. Grant and the
Union armies on the present day cele-
no effect on the present day celebration of this all-American holiday.
It is a fact that past generations
...stant to recognize the
Fourth, and
...dence

their mules and horses
meat, lined the street
parade went by but th...
cheering, no confetti—
missive bitterness.
Nearly every pers...
nessed the events of
passed on. Time h...
wounds of this a...
and younger g...
again recognized the tr...
of Independence Day.
A general holiday will be observed here Friday. The Retail
Merchants Association has voted to
close stores; and a majority of of-
...public buildings will be

GENERAL DWIGHT D. EISENHOWER
GENERAL OF THE ARMIES
Honor Guest of the third annual
CARNIVAL OF THE CONFEDERACY

VICKSBURG REJOINS THE UNION

A land without ruins is a land without memories—a land without memories is a land without history. A land that wears a laurel crown may be fair to see; but twine a few sad cypress leaves around the brow. . . . and it wins the sympathy of the heart and of history. Crowns of roses fade—crowns of thorns endure.

—"A Land Without Ruins"
Fr. Abram J. Ryan
priest and poet, 1895

Epilogue

It took only two hours on a spring morning in 1876 for the surging, foaming, brown waters of the Mississippi River to cut a wide swath across the peninsula opposite Vicksburg, and by nightfall, steamboats were passing through the new channel. The River City no longer had a waterfront.

Only thirteen years before, the same feat had been attempted by Grant's men, who, after several efforts, many months, and with the best equipment, had failed. Now nature had done it in the twinkling of an eye, and the route was not the one attempted by Union forces.

Vicksburg residents may have noted the date and wondered if there was a message in the timing: it was April 26, one day before Grant's fifty-fourth birthday.

The change in the course of the river was only one of many events that were reminders of the war years, of the time when Vicksburg had met its date with destiny.

The conclusion of hostilities brought mixed reactions from the

Funeral Notice.

The public generally and especially the friends of both wings of the "late lamented"

RADICAL PARTY,

also the friends of Speed, Fisk, Furlong, Mygatt, Lease, & Co., are earnestly and cordially invited to attend the funeral of the deceased, to take place from its late residence corner of Washington and Jackson Streets, this (SATURDAY) evening, at half-past 7 o'clock—precisely.

VICKSBURG, July 11th, 1868.

The members of the Loyal League are requested to assemble at 7 o'clock this evening. to take part in the funeral obsequies of their late (so-called) friend. Punctuality is requested as the advanced state of decomposition renders the remains obnoxious.

P. S.—This sudden and unlooked for demise having so completely overwhelmed the family of the deceased with grief unutterable, renders them unable to perform the last sad rites; the funeral services will. therefore, be conducted by kind members of the opposite party.

A notice for a mock funeral celebrated the temporary defeat of the carpetbaggers and scalawags who controlled Vicksburg in 1868. (OCHM)

people. Many, no doubt, were war weary and just glad it was over, regardless of the outcome. Some opted to start anew in other lands, such as South and Central America, and some bedraggled Confederates literally had nothing to lose and moved on to Wyoming and Montana and California. Local Unionists probably echoed the sentiments of Dora Miller, who had said in 1863 after the siege, when she saw the Stars and Stripes flying over the courthouse, "Once again I feel at home in my own country." Most Vicksburgers, regardless of political sentiments, stayed in their hometown and, whether grudgingly or otherwise, accepted the results and determined to take their places in a country reunited, even if it had been put together again by the sword. Many Northerners understandably doubted the sincerity of the former Confederates, but a Union veteran came to their assistance: Sgt. Gilbert H. Bates of Wisconsin bet that he could carry the United States flag through the Southern states without harm, that he would in fact be cheered. Bates began his trek in Vicksburg on the morning of January 24, 1868. Though once a foe, he was now a guest of the city, and a tremendous throng gave him an enthusiastic sendoff from the site of Pemberton and Grant's surrender talks. Bates met with a similar reception all across the South, receiving his only rebuff when he tried to enter the capitol building in Washington.

Under Federal rules and scrutiny, local governments were organized, and during the coming years, residents contended with various plans of reconstruction. Eventually, in 1870, Mississippi was readmitted to the Union—proof, it would seem, that the state had indeed seceded despite Northern political dogma that there could be no such thing.

Gradually, the garrison was reduced until, by the mid-1870s, only a token number of soldiers remained. The era had seen the reins of government wrested, often violently, from carpetbagger rule. In 1874 veterans who had worn blue stood shoulder to shoulder with the sons of the South in securing political control of Vicksburg.

The war was still fresh in the minds of the men who fought it and the women who encouraged them when veterans of the 3rd Louisiana Infantry unveiled a monument in memory of their comrades killed at Vicksburg; The unit had suffered the highest percentage of casualties of any Confederate regiment involved in the siege. The beautiful marble memorial was placed in the green on Monroe Street in downtown Vicksburg in 1885; it was the first Confederate memorial in the city.

The land on the outskirts of town, where the two armies had faced each other for forty-seven days, still bore scars. On the edge of the rugged battlefield was a terraced and manicured national cemetery where almost 18,000 Union men were buried, and not far away, within the city's Cedar Hill Cemetery, was another graveyard, Soldiers' Rest, where the fallen Confederates were interred, their graves tended by a group of patriotic ladies.

Each year more and more veterans, from both sides, came to reflect and reminisce about their roles in what was (so many thought) the turning point of the war. In 1890 a national reunion of the gray and blue was held at Vicksburg, and it wasn't long before efforts were begun to create a national military park. The idea began to take shape when Tom Lewis, a Vicksburg citizen who enjoyed showing the hallowed ground to visitors, began circulating petitions. Soon some of the veterans joined in the effort, and an organization was formed to secure the goal. In 1899, Pres. William McKinley signed into law the measure that created the Vicksburg National Military Park. With renewed zeal, the men told their personal experiences, gave individual and invaluable input as to what

Veterans of the 3rd Louisiana Infantry erected this monument on Monroe Street in 1885. It was the first such commemoration in Vicksburg. (OCHM)

[See page 152.]

149

MOURNERS APPLAUDED PRIEST'S PRAYER

Father Picherit

Upon the death of Jefferson Davis on December 7, 1889, the bell on the old Warren County Court House began tolling around two in the afternoon; soon the church bells of the city joined, and they rang until dark.

Four days later, on the day of the funeral (which was held in New Orleans), the columns of the local newspapers were bordered in black, and the Court House, Christ Church, and stores in Vicksburg were draped in mourning.

At a memorial service Davis' hometown friends filled the opera house to overflowing. On the program were several Protestant ministers, a Jewish rabbi (who was from the North), and a Roman Catholic priest who had been a Confederate chaplain. A choir sang appropriate numbers, public officials spoke in tribute to the deceased hero, the rabbi read a poem he had composed for the occasion, and Colonel R. V. Booth delivered an eloquent eulogy.

It was the priest, Father Picherit, however, who made the most memorable impression on the crowd. His prayer began conventionally enough but turned midway into such a moving farewell to the man whose faith in the justice of the Lost Cause had never wavered, that he had men and women alike in tears. When his voice rang out proudly with the phrase ". . . and went to his grave undaunted and unreconstructed," there was a sudden burst of loud applause. Just as suddenly they grew silent, seeming to have been embarrassed that this was a prayer during a sorrowful and solemn occasion.

Appropriate or not, there could not have been a warmer or more sincere tribute from Jefferson Davis' hometown citizens than their spontaneous approval for the man who had refused to apologize for leading the Cause which they still considered a righteous one.

—*Vicksburg Daily Herald*
December 7 and 12, 1889

*. . . and went
to his grave undaunted
and unreconstructed*

Jefferson Davis as he appeared shortly before his death in 1889. (Jones: *Davis Memorial Volume*)

had happened back in 1863, and the land where Americans battled each other became what is one of the best-marked battlefields in the world, a permanent reminder of the past.

Old wounds heal slowly; however, and years before, on a March day in 1885, residents were startled when the booming of cannons rattled windows and smoke covered the dock downtown (in flood season the river flowed temporarily in front of the city). Briefly, those who remembered were reminded of the bombardment in 1862. When the smoke cleared, the Stars and Stripes could be seen fluttering over the deck of the steamboat *Natchez*. Capt. Thomas Paul Leathers, a Confederate stalwart and holdout, had finally forgiven the Yankees and rejoined the Union. It had taken him a quarter century to bury the hatchet, but only then because Grover Cleveland, a Democrat, was inaugurated president on that day.

Half a century after the last shot was fired, there remained a bit of a stigma attached to the blue uniform, and even the opportunity to appear in a movie had its price. When guardsmen were hired as extras to portray Northern and Southern troops in *The Crisis,* a film made in Vicksburg in 1917 and the first in Mississippi, those who donned Yankee garb had to be paid twice as much as the men who wore gray.

On many occasions Vicksburg citizens remembered and paid their last respects, but it was an especially sad time in December 1889, when public buildings were draped in mourning and bells tolled for hours, sounding the city's grief for her most famous son, Jefferson Davis.

As long as there were veterans, as long as some who remembered were able, events commemorating the South's heroic and historic struggle were grand occasions with parades and speeches and marching bands, but each year, the reunions were smaller as the older generation faded into the past. It was on April 22, 1939,

In 1892 a monument was dedicated in Cedar Hill Cemetery by the Vicksburg chapter of the United Daughters of the Confederacy. (OCHM)

only four days before Confederate Memorial Day, that Louis Hornthal, Vicksburg's last Confederate veteran, died.

An era had ended, but Vicksburg had not forgotten—nor completely forgiven. For eighty years the nation's birthday, the Fourth of July, had passed quietly and without public notice, though the day was often a time for family outings and picnics. With successes on two fronts, as World War II was coming to a close, a thankful people decided it was time to stage a gala, complete with bands and parades, flags, and speeches. The date was July 4, 1945, and Vicksburg's decision to celebrate the fourth was broadcast around the world. The story would be repeated for several years, with the grandest event taking place in 1947, when Gen. Dwight D. Eisenhower was the city's guest of honor.

After all those years, however, the city's final surrender wasn't unconditional—the festival was billed as the "Carnival of the Confederacy." Vicksburg had at long last rejoined the Union—but she was still looking over her shoulder.

On May 22, 1937, the anniversary of the final and failed Union assault on Vicksburg, grandsons of the commanding generals met at the surrender monument. On the left is John C. Pemberton, III, shaking hands with U. S. Grant, III. (OCHM)

PHOTOGRAPH CREDITS

Though credit is given at the end of each cutline, there are some individuals and organizations we wish to thank for their generosity in sharing photographs.

Bryan Brabston, Vicksburg, MS
Kent Masterson Brown and Wood Simpson, Lexington, KY
Civil War Times Illustrated
Patrick T. Dolan, Denver, CO
Betty Jean Wright Lanier, Sardis, MS
Michael J. McAfee, curator of history, West Point Military
 Museum, West Point, NY
Laurier McDonald, Edenburg, TX
Library of Congress, Washington, DC
Merle and Cathy Messerschmidt, East Troy, WI
United States Military History Institute, Carlisle Barracks, PA

We also appreciate the help of Bob Pickett of Pickett Photography
 in Vicksburg and C. Todd Sherman of the *Vicksburg Post,* and
 James M. "Sonny" Watt of Vicksburg.

John Benjamin Wright of Yokena, south of Vicksburg, was a member of Charlton's Independent Company, which later became Company K, 45th Mississippi Infantry. He was wounded at the Battle of Murfreesboro, Tennessee, on December 31, 1862. (Betty Jean Wright Lanier)

BIBLIOGRAPHY

Adams, Matthew R. Letter to Sister. 31 January 1863. A copy is in the collections of the Old Court House Museum, Vicksburg, MS.

Bachman, Robert L. Memoir. A copy is in the collections of the Old Court House Museum, Vicksburg, MS, donated by Mrs. Lewis Rumford, II, of Baltimore, MD.

Bearss, Edwin C., and Warren E. Grabau. *The Battle of Jackson, the Siege of Jackson, and Three Other Post-Vicksburg Actions.* Baltimore, MD: Gateway Press, 1981.

Bearss, Edwin C. *The Vicksburg Campaign.* 3 vols. Dayton, OH: Morningside House, 1986.

Biographical Directory of the American Congress 1774-1927. United States Government Printing Office, 1928.

Bradley, George. Diary. A copy is in the collections of the Old Court House Museum, Vicksburg, MS, donated by Cathy Cox of Colorado Springs, CO.

Bragg, Marion B. *St. Alban's Episcopal Church.* Vicksburg, MS: Privately published by Hammer Memorial Library, 1963.

Browne, Junius Henri. *Four Years in Secessia.* Hartford, CN: D. Case and Company, 1865.

Carter, Samuel, III. *The Final Fortress.* New York: St. Martin's Press, 1980.

Austin Augustus Trescott posed for this painting holding the flag of the 21st Mississippi Infantry. He served in the Volunteer Southrons, Company A of the regiment, and was captured at Sayler's Creek, Virginia, on April 6, 1865. The flag and painting are on display at the Old Court House Museum. (C. Todd Sherman)

Chance, Joseph E. *The Second Texas Infantry*. Austin, TX: Eakin Press, 1984.

Cotton, Gordon A. *Antioch: The First Baptist Church in Warren County, Mississippi*. Vicksburg, MS: Privately published, 1997.

——. "Minister Tells Story of Whistling Dick's Demise." *Vicksburg Sunday Post* (October 12, 1986).

——. *Yankee Bullets, Rebel Rations*. Raymond, MS: Keith Printing Company, 1984.

——, and Ralph C. Mason. *With Malice Toward Some*. Vicksburg, MS: Office Supply Company, 1991.

Cunningham, P. E. *A History of the First Baptist Church, Vicksburg, Mississippi*. Raymond, MS: Keith Press, 1964.

Davis, William C. *The Orphan Brigade*. Garden City, NJ: Doubleday and Company, 1980.

Esposito, Vincent J., ed. *The West Point Atlas of American Wars*. 2 vols. New York: Frederick A. Praeger, 1959.

Everett, Frank E., Jr. *A History of the First Presbyterian Church of Vicksburg, Mississippi in the Nineteenth Century*. Np: Privately published, 1980.

Faulk, William L. Diary; 18 May 1863-9 July 1863; 38th Mississippi File, Vicksburg National Military Park, Vicksburg, MS.

Cpl. Augustus A. Folkes posed with his brothers for this painting, circa 1861. He was a member of Company G, 1st Mississippi Light Artillery and was the son of Vicksburg mayor Miles C. Folkes. (OCHM)

Fulkerson, H. S. *A Civilian's Recollections of the War Between the States.* Baton Rouge, LA: Otto Claitor, 1939.

Giambrone, Jeff T. *Beneath Torn and Tattered Flags: A History of the 38th Mississippi Infantry.* Np: Privately Published, 1998.

Grabau, Warren E. *Ninety-Eight Days.* Knoxville, TN: University of Tennessee Press, 2000.

Grant, Ulysses S. *Personal Memoirs of U. S. Grant.* 2 vols. New York: Charles L. Webster and Company, 1885.

Griffin, Patrick M. "The Famous Tenth Tennessee." *Confederate Veteran* 555 (December 1905).

Headley, J. T. *The Great Rebellion.* 2 vols. Hartford, CN: American Publishing Company, 1866.

Headley, Katy McCaleb. *Claiborne County, Mississippi: The Promised Land.* Baton Rouge, LA: Moran Industries, 1976.

Horton, R. G. A. *Youth's History of the Great Civil War in the United States.* New York: Van Evrie, Horton and Company, 1866.

Howard, R. L. *History of the 124th Illinois Infantry Volunteers.* Springfield, IL: H. W. Rokker, 1880.

Illinois at Vicksburg. Published under authority of an act of the Forty-Fifth General Assembly by the Illinois-Vicksburg Military Commission, 1907.

Nathaniel Hoggatt served as a third lieutenant in Gibbs Confederate Guards, a Warren County unit that became Company C of the 21st Tennessee Infantry. He was wounded in action at the Battle of Shiloh in April 1862. (Bryan Brabston)

Jones, James H. "The Rank and File at Vicksburg." Publications of the Mississippi Historical Society, vol. 7 (1903): 17-31.

Jones, John G. *A Complete History of Methodism.* Baton Rouge, LA: Claitor's Book Store, 1966.

Kidd, James T. Memoir. A copy is in the collections of the Old Court House Museum, Vicksburg, MS, donated by Robert L. Kidd of Ecru, MS.

Kilgore, Nettie. *The History of Columbia County, Arkansas.* Np., n.d.

Loughborough, Mary. *My Cave Life in Vicksburg.* New York: D. Appleton and Company, 1864.

Miller, Dora Richards. "War Diary of a Union Woman in the South." *The Century Illustrated Monthly Magazine,* 38, New Series vol. 16 (May 1889-October 1889). A complete copy of the diary is owned by Bonnie Gunsaulus of Baton Rouge, LA.

Moneyhon, Carl, and Bobby Roberts. *Portraits of Conflict: A Photographic History of Mississippi in the Civil War.* Fayetteville, AR: University of Arkansas Press, 1993.

Mottelay, Paul F., ed. *The Soldier in Our Civil War.* 2 vols. New York: J. H. Brown Publishing Company, 1884.

Oakes, Sr. Mary Paulinus. *Angels of Mercy: An Eyewitness Account of the Civil War and Yellow Fever.* Baltimore, MD: Cathedral Foundation Press, 1998.

Ragland, Mary Lois S., comp. *Fisher Funeral Home Records Vicksburg, Mississippi 1854-1867.* Bowie, MD: Heritage Books, 1992.

Rand, Clayton. *Stars in Their Eyes: Dreamers and Builders of Louisiana.* Gulfport, MS: Dixie Press, 1953.

Pvt. Walter W. Adams of the Volunteer Southrons, Company A, 21st Mississippi Infantry, fought in most of the major engagements in the eastern theatre of the war as part of the Army of Northern Virginia. Badly wounded at the battle of Cedar Creek, Virginia, on October 19, 1864, he was found in a Northern hospital by his brother-in-law, James W. Goodrum, and brought home to Warren County. (OCHM)

Richardson, Albert D. *The Secret Service, the Field, the Dungeon, and the Escape.* Hartford, CN: American Publishing Company, 1865.

Sherman, William T. *Memoirs of General W. T. Sherman.* 2 vols. New York: D. Appleton and Company, 1875.

Slack, A. L. *Louisiana's Part in the Vicksburg Siege.* Unpublished memoir, 1906. A copy is in the collections of the Old Court House Museum, Vicksburg, MS, donated by Torbert Slack of Lake Charles, LA.

Smith, George E. Letter to James A. McKenzie. 6 May 1863. A copy is in the collections of the Old Court House Museum, Vicksburg, MS, donated by Al and Leah Nummer of Reno, NV.

United States War Department, comp. *War of the Rebellion: Official Records of the Union and Confederate Armies.* 73 vols. 128 parts. Washington, DC: 1880-1902.

Urquhart, Kenneth Trist, ed. *Vicksburg: Southern City Under Siege.* New Orleans: Historic New Orleans Collection, 1980.

Vicksburg (Mississippi) Daily Citizen.

Walker, Peter F. *Vicksburg: A People at War, 1860-1865.* Chapel Hill, NC: University of North Carolina Press, 1960.

Warner, Ezra J. *Generals in Blue.* Baton Rouge, LA: Louisiana State University Press, 1964.

———. *Generals in Gray.* Baton Rouge, LA: Louisiana State University Press, 1959.

William Tell Keller, born in Canada of Swiss parents, lived east of Vicksburg at Mount Alban. He served in the Crystal Springs Southern Rights, Company C, 16th Mississippi Infantry. He was captured during the Battle of Weldon Railroad at Petersburg, Virginia, on August 21, 1864. (OCHM)

Gen. Thomas Waul of Texas and Gen. Stephen D. Lee of South Carolina posed for a reunion photo December 11, 1901, at Vicksburg. Both fought in the Vicksburg campaign; Waul had lived in Vicksburg as a young man and Lee late in life. (OCHM)

"We are stragglers in the great march. The victory is already won, and our comrades expect our coming to share the glory of their triumph. In the little time left us before we report to our Great Commander, let us acquit ourselves like men. When the pale sergeant comes we shall listen to voices in the upper air saying 'Welcome, comrade! Do they love us still in Dixie?'"

—Gen. Stephen D. Lee